S. HRG. 114–75

SAFEGUARDING AMERICAN INTERESTS IN THE EAST AND SOUTH CHINA SEAS

HEARING

BEFORE THE

COMMITTEE ON FOREIGN RELATIONS UNITED STATES SENATE

ONE HUNDRED FOURTEENTH CONGRESS

FIRST SESSION

MAY 13, 2015

Printed for the use of the Committee on Foreign Relations

Available via the World Wide Web: http://www.gpo.gov/fdsys/

U.S. GOVERNMENT PUBLISHING OFFICE

96–850 PDF   WASHINGTON : 2015

For sale by the Superintendent of Documents, U.S. Government Publishing Office
Internet: bookstore.gpo.gov   Phone: toll free (866) 512–1800; DC area (202) 512–1800
Fax: (202) 512–2104   Mail: Stop IDCC, Washington, DC 20402–0001

(II)

CONTENTS

SAFEGUARDING AMERICAN INTERESTS IN THE EAST AND SOUTH CHINA SEAS

WEDNESDAY, MAY 13, 2015

U.S. SENATE,
COMMITTEE ON FOREIGN RELATIONS,
Washington, DC.

The committee met, pursuant to notice, at 2:16 p.m., in room SD–419, Dirksen Senate Office Building, Hon. Bob Corker (chairman of the committee) presiding.

Present: Senator Corker, Gardner, Perdue, Cardin, and Murphy.

OPENING STATEMENT OF HON. BOB CORKER, U.S. SENATOR FROM TENNESSEE

The CHAIRMAN. I will call the meeting to order.

In June 2014, this committee held a hearing on the future of United States-China relations. At that time, I raised concerns over the lack of a coherent China policy, including the absence of sustained high-level engagement from senior administration officials despite the consistent rhetoric that the United States-China relationship is one of the most consequential relationships for United States political, security, and economic interests.

I left that hearing scratching my head. And after nearly a year later, I am even more troubled.

Yesterday, this committee convened to discuss a new nuclear cooperation agreement with China. We heard troubling information about the Chinese intent to divert U.S. technology for military purposes. In addition, we were told that China has not taken adequate steps to end proliferation of sensitive technologies by Chinese entities and individuals to countries of concern, including Iran and North Korea.

Despite these concerns, administration officials testified in support of a new nuclear cooperation agreement, noting the mutual benefits for the bilateral relationship, including commercial interests.

This afternoon, the absence of a genuine China policy will be on display as we discuss the situation in the East and South China Seas where China continues to engage in provocative and destabilizing behavior.

As you can see from these pictures on display, China continues to engage in land reclamation and construction activities, the scope and scale of which are unprecedented in the South China Sea.

Figure 1 shows Fiery Cross Reef, in the Spratly Islands, as it appeared on May 2014. Figure 2 shows that same reef less than a year later with over 1,300 meters of runway already completed and analyst assessments that it could be expanded up to 3,100 meters.

Clearly, these activities are not simply limited to dredging and piling sand. China is deliberately constructing facilities on these reefs and islets that could be used for military purposes, including airstrips and ports, as you can see in Figure 3, which shows Fiery Cross Reef just a few weeks ago. Again, in Figure 4, you can see large, multistory buildings with additional military capabilities.

Moreover, Beijing has publicly confirmed that there are military uses for these facilities, with China's foreign ministry spokesperson stating on March 9 that this construction was undertaken in part to satisfy the necessary military defense needs.

It is worth noting that all of these activities are occurring against the backdrop of China's massive military buildup, including significant investments in the antiaccess/area-denial capabilities.

Most China watchers believe that Beijing does not want to start a conflict in either the East or South China Seas. Yet many of the same experts concede that Beijing may do everything short of engaging in a military conflict to solidify its claims.

That is why I recently joined Senators McCain, Reed, and Menendez in a bipartisan letter to Secretary Kerry and Secretary Carter to highlight our growing concerns with China's efforts to alter the status quo through ongoing land reclamation and construction activities in the South China Sea.

According to the most recent statistics, some $5 trillion in global ship-borne trade passes through the South China Sea annually. As you can see from Figure 5, all of the major trade routes through the South China Sea pass near disputed areas in both the Spratlys and Paracels. And you can see those circled on this display.

I hope we will be able to have a thoughtful discussion today that outlines U.S. interests in the Indo-Pacific and how Chinese actions in the East and South China Seas affect, if at all, the balance of the United States-China bilateral relationship.

In addition, I hope we will explore various options available to the United States to ensure that the situation in the East and South China Seas does not result in a conflict. I support efforts to constructively engage with China, including strengthening economic and trade ties.

Yet simply defaulting to an approach that maintains cooperation while managing differences with China is not a successful formula, particularly when such management cedes United States influence and places American interests at risk in the Indo-Pacific.

I am concerned that absent a course correction, specifically high-level and dedicated engagement from the United States Government to articulate a coherent China policy, our credibility will continue to suffer throughout the region, whether it is in regards to nonproliferation or preserving freedom of navigation in the East and South China Seas.

I look forward to hearing from the witnesses and thank them for being here.

And now I look forward to hearing from our distinguished ranking member.

OPENING STATEMENT OF HON. BENJAMIN L. CARDIN, U.S. SENATOR FROM MARYLAND

Senator CARDIN. Well, thank you, Chairman Corker. I appreciate you very much holding this hearing. This is a very, very important hearing.

The relationship between the United States and China is critically important to this country. It is a complex relationship.

Yesterday, we held a hearing on our civil nuclear cooperation, and I thought that hearing brought out many points that were extremely important to follow up on. Today's hearing dealing with the security in the South China Sea and East China Sea is equally important, and China plays a critical role in regard to maritime security issues.

So it is a very important hearing, and I thank you for conducting this.

There are clearly differences in the claims of territorial rights in the China seas. The important thing, though, is to have an effective mechanism to deal with maritime disputes. That needs to be our key policy objective. And I know President Obama has underscored the importance of effective mechanisms for dealing with the maritime disputes.

Provocative conduct is not helpful at all, and we have seen more and more of these provocative incidents. China, particularly, has been very much responsible for taking actions that make the circumstances much more dangerous.

Ambassador Shear, when I was in Vietnam, that was the most important issue that was brought up to me, the concern that Vietnam's future was very much at risk due to the oil rig activity that China was doing in areas that Vietnam had reasonable rights to make claims that that was their territory.

Unilateral action by China caused a major problem at the time that could have escalated even more than it did. But that was not the only time. The reclamation efforts that Senator Corker is talking about, in an effort to gain more territorial and maritime claims, is a provocative action by China today.

You mentioned Fiery Cross, where construction and reclamation has increased the size by elevenfold since August of last year. We can also talk about Gaven Reef, where 14,000 square meters have been constructed since March 2014, or Johnson Reef, where there have been 100,000 square meters in an area that was submerged before, all this in an effort to really change the equation in the region by taking unilateral actions.

What this does is it clearly affects the stability of the region and jeopardizes the free flow of commerce. So the United States has a direct interest in this and we must do everything we can to resolve these issues peacefully.

China is not the only country that has taken provocative action, but they are the largest. And they are the ones who have been the most bold in taking these actions. There are conflicts over overlapping territorial claims by nations in the region, with China, the Philippines, Brunei, Malaysia, and Vietnam also making claims, often conflicting, to islands, reefs, and shoals in the South China Sea. And then there are China and Taiwan also asserting their rights, a whole lot of them through expansive nine-dash line territorial claims.

In the East China Sea, it is clear United States policy that although we do not take a position on the ultimate sovereignty of the Senkaku Islands, the Senkakus are under Japan's administrative control, and we oppose unilateral efforts by third parties to change the status quo. Nonetheless, China has asserted a claim to the Senkakus.

So what can we do? And what should the United States be doing? First and foremost, we believe it is essential for all parties to exercise self-restraint to avoid making the situation worse.

The use of coercion, threats, or force to assert disputed claims in the region or to seek a change in the current status quo is just not acceptable.

We have been working with the ASEAN organization to develop a code of conduct for resolving maritime disputes. It is not clear whether China will participate or not. They certainly have not been cooperative in developing a code of conduct that would allow for the rule of law, orderly processes to deal with disputes and not taking unilateral action.

I think it is important that we continue to urge the ASEAN members to come up with a code of conduct, a gold standard for resolving these issues, even if China does not participate. We will at least have a gold standard for how to deal with this.

I think we need to redouble our efforts to work with the Asia-Pacific region to develop a functional problem-solving architecture that could support the resolution of disputes through a collaborative diplomatic process consistent with the recognized principles of international law.

Let me also point out there are other things that we can do. The United States can play a significant role in bolstering the region's maritime security capacity, including maritime domain awareness, and help contribute to effective regional management of maritime security issues.

Finally, the United States must continue to demonstrate an enduring commitment to the region and an enduring presence there.

We will stand by our treaty allies. We will deepen our partnership in the region. And we will continue the operations by our Armed Forces in support of freedom of navigation, the maintenance of peace and stability, and respect of international law.

Mr. Chairman, let me just say lastly, it may not be directly on point, but I do think the fact that we have never ratified the Law of the Sea Treaty does not give us the full standing in this area where we could have a strong position. I know that there is controversy, which I do not fully understand, but I do believe that the United States has been a leader in maritime security issues. And our presence in the China seas is critically important to maintain stability.

I just think we would have stronger standing if we would join other nations that have already ratified the Law of the Sea Treaty, and that would give us an even stronger standing.

I want to welcome both of our witnesses here today. Secretary Russel and I worked together in the last Congress when I chaired the East Asia and Pacific Subcommittee that Senator Gardner now chairs. Secretary Russel has been an incredibly valuable partner with us in the rebalance to Asia, and we thank you very much for your help.

And Ambassador Shear has been a great servant of the public and now in his position as Assistant Secretary of Defense.

It is a pleasure to have both of you before our committee.

The CHAIRMAN Thank you for those comments.

I would never want to get in a tit-for-tat with the outstanding ranking member, who I respect so much and enjoy working with. I will say that China is a signatory to the Law of the Sea Treaty and it does not seem to be having a very positive effect, so I do not know that you can say one plus one equals two, in that particular case.

Senator CARDIN. I do not want to argue with my chairman, but if we were to ratify it, we might be able to use that mechanism more effectively with China.

The CHAIRMAN Yes, I got it.

Anyway, thank you so much.

Our first witness is the Honorable Danny Russel, Assistant Secretary for East Asian and Pacific Affairs. We thank you for being here, and thank you for your service to our country.

Our second witness, the Honorable David Shear, Assistant Secretary of Defense for Asian and Pacific Security Affairs. We also thank you for being here, and thank you for your public service.

If you will, I think you know the drill, make some brief comments that you think are very important to our discussion openly here today. Your entire testimony will be entered into the record, and we look forward to the Q&A. Thank you very much.

STATEMENT OF THE HON. DANIEL R. RUSSEL, ASSISTANT SECRETARY OF STATE FOR EAST ASIAN AND PACIFIC AFFAIRS, U.S. DEPARTMENT OF STATE, WASHINGTON, DC

Mr. RUSSEL. Mr. Chairman, thank you very much, and Senator Cardin, Senator Gardner. I appreciate the opportunity to testify today with my good friend and colleague, Dave Shear.

I thank you also for this committee's strong bipartisan support of our work in the East Asia and Pacific region.

The East and the South China Seas are important to global commerce and regional stability. So the handling of the territorial and maritime issues in these waters has economic and security consequences for the United States. And while disputes have existed there for decades, tensions have increased in the last several years.

Not only could a serious incident provoke a dangerous escalatory cycle, but the region's efforts to develop a stable, rules-based order are also challenged by coercive behavior.

This gives the United States a vested interest in ensuring that disputes are managed peacefully. Our strategy aims to preserve space for diplomatic solutions by pressing all claimants to exercise restraint, maintain open channels of dialogue, lower rhetoric, clarify their claims in accordance with international law, and behave responsibly at sea and in the air.

Mr. Chairman, the United States strongly opposes the threat or the use of force or coercion of any kind, and we are concerned about assertive behavior, as we saw in the standoff following China's deployment of an oil rig in disputed waters off the coast of Vietnam last year; as we saw in several incidents involving the Philippines and China; and as we are seeing in China's land reclamation and construction, which, as you pointed out, dwarfs that of any other claimant.

This ongoing activity raises regional tensions. It does nothing to strengthen China's legal claims. It runs counter to past agreements with ASEAN. And it also harms the environment.

China's arguments and justifications have not alleviated its neighbors concerns. Only halting these activities, negotiating a binding code of conduct with ASEAN, and clarifying the claims in accordance with international law will lead to stability and good regional relations.

We recognize it takes time for sovereignty disputes to be resolved. In the meantime, we are working for peace, stability, and for our national interests.

Here is how. First, we are ensuring that maritime issues are at the top of the agenda in the region's multilateral fora, showing that the entire region is concerned. And I will host a conference on Friday with the senior officials from all 10 of the Southeast Asian ASEAN countries.

Second, we are shining a spotlight on problematic behavior, including land reclamation, to ensure that destabilizing behavior is exposed and addressed.

Third, we are defending the right to dispute settlement under law, including binding arbitration under the Law of the Sea Convention. Much of the region now accepts that as a valid way to deal with disputes when diplomatic negotiations have not succeeded.

Fourth, we are forging cooperative partnerships with Southeast Asian coastal states to improve their maritime domain awareness so they know what is happening off the shores.

Fifth, we are coordinating closely with allies like Japan and Australia to maximize the impact of our assistance and diplomacy.

Sixth, we are encouraging information-sharing and consultations so that all countries seeking peaceful resolution operate from a common situational picture.

Seventh, we are talking directly and at senior levels. For instance, President Obama has engaged President Xi of China candidly on maritime disputes. His message is clear: China should build common ground through diplomacy in the region, not artificial ground through dredging in the South China Sea.

And lastly, we maintain an enduring and formidable security presence, which my colleague, Dave Shear, will address in a moment. It is lost on nobody that our alliances and our military footprint in East Asia deter conflict and help keep the peace in this important region.

So, Mr. Chairman, our strategy and our actions are designed to protect rules, not protect rocks. We are working to protect U.S. national security, U.S. interests, to maintain the peace, to sustain freedom, to strengthen the rule of law, to deter aggression, to prevent coercion, to lower tensions and risk, and to encourage the claimants and the parties in the region to work together peacefully.

Thank you very much.

[The prepared statement of Mr. Russel follows:]

PREPARED STATEMENT OF DANIEL RUSSEL

MARITIME ISSUES IN EAST ASIA

Mr. Chairman, members of the committee, thank you for the opportunity to appear before you today to testify with David Shear, Assistant Secretary of Defense for the Asia-Pacific, on this very important and timely topic. I would also like to thank the committee for its leadership in supporting and promoting bipartisan engagement with the Asia-Pacific and advancing U.S. interests there. You have demonstrated that this committee understands the importance of the Asia-Pacific region to U.S. national security.

Over the last 6 years, the Obama administration has established a "new normal" of U.S. relations with the Asia-Pacific region, consisting of extensive collaboration with Asian allies and partners on important economic, security, and other global issues as well as a high tempo of sustained engagement by the President, Secretary Kerry, me and my team, and other Cabinet and senior officials. Over the course of this calendar year, we will have held 41 bilateral, 5 trilateral, and 54 multilateral dialogues and high level meetings on a range of policy issues. We welcomed Prime Minister Abe last month, and President Obama will host several leaders from the region later this year, including from the Republic of Korea, China, and Indonesia.

At the same time we are meeting ongoing crises and challenges elsewhere in the world, we are systematically implementing a comprehensive diplomatic, economic, and security strategy in Asia. At the heart of our rebalance is a determination to ensure that the Asia-Pacific remains an open, inclusive, and prosperous region guided by widely accepted rules and standards and adherence to international law. This is clearly in the interest of our own national security, as developments in 21st-century Asia will reverberate throughout the world and here at home.

For nearly 70 years, the United States, along with our allies and partners, has helped to sustain in Asia a maritime regime, based on international law, which has underpinned the region's stability and remarkable economic growth. International law makes clear the legal basis on which states can legitimately assert their rights in the maritime domain or exploit marine resources. By promoting order in the seas, international law has been instrumental in safeguarding the rights and freedoms of all countries regardless of size or military strength. We have an abiding interest in freedom of navigation and overflight and other internationally lawful uses of the sea related to those freedoms in the East and South China Seas and around the world.

The East and South China Seas are important to global commerce and regional stability. Their economic and strategic significance means that the handling of territorial and maritime issues in these waters by various parties could have economic and security consequences for U.S. national interests. While disputes have existed for decades, tensions have increased considerably in the last several years. One of our concerns has been the possibility that a miscalculation or incident could touch off an escalatory cycle that would be difficult to defuse. The effects of a crisis would be felt around the world.

This gives the United States a vested interest in ensuring that territorial and maritime issues are managed peacefully. Our strategy aims to preserve space for diplomatic solutions, including by pressing all claimants to exercise restraint, maintain open channels of dialogue, lower rhetoric, behave responsibly at sea and in the air and acknowledge that the same rules and standards apply to all claimants, without regard for size or strength. We strongly oppose the threat of force or use of force or coercion by any claimant.

East China Sea

Let me begin with the situation in the East China Sea. Notwithstanding any competing sovereignty claims, Japan has administered the Senkaku Islands since the 1972 reversion of Okinawa to Japan. As such, they fall under Article V of the U.S.-Japan Security Treaty. With ships and aircraft operating in close proximity to the Senkakus, extreme caution is needed to reduce the risk of an accident or incident. We strongly discourage any actions in the East China Sea that could increase tensions and encourage the use of peaceful means and diplomacy. In this regard, we welcome the resumed high-level dialogue between China and Japan and the restart of talks on crisis management mechanisms. We hope that this will translate into a more peaceful and stable environment in the East China Sea.

South China Sea

Disputes regarding sovereignty over land features and resource rights in the Asia-Pacific region, including the South China Sea, have been around for a long time. Some of these disputes have led to open conflict such as those over the Paracel Islands in 1974 and Johnson South Reef in 1988. While we have not witnessed another conflict like those in recent years, the increasing frequency of incidents in the South China Sea highlights the need for all countries to move quickly in finding peaceful, diplomatic approaches to address these disputes.

We know that this is possible. There are instances throughout the region where neighbors have peacefully resolved differences over overlapping maritime zones. Recent examples include Indonesia's and the Philippines' successful conclusion of negotiations to delimit the boundary between their respective exclusive economic zones (EEZs) and India's and Bangladesh's decision to accept the decision of an arbitral tribunal with regard to their overlapping EEZ in the Bay of Bengal. There have also been instances where claimants have agreed to shelve the disputes and find peaceful ways to manage resources in contested areas. In its approach to the East China Sea, Taiwan forged a landmark fishing agreement with Japan through cooperative dispute resolution. These examples should be emulated.

All disputes over claims in the South China Sea should be pursued, addressed, and resolved peacefully. In our view, there are several acceptable ways for claimants to handle these disputes. In the first instance, claimants should use negotiations to try and resolve the competing sovereignty claims over land features and competing claims to maritime resources. However, the fact remains that if every claimant continues to hold a position that their respective territorial and maritime claims are "indisputable," that leaves parties with very little room for compromise. In addition, mutually agreeable solutions to jointly manage or exploit marine resources are more difficult to find if not all claimants are basing their claims on the Law of the Sea. Another reasonable option would be for claimants to submit their maritime claims to arbitration by a neutral third party to assess the validity of their claims. The Philippines, for example, is seeking clarification from an international tribunal on the validity of China's nine-dash line as a maritime claim under the United Nations Law of the Sea Convention, as well as greater clarity over what types of maritime entitlements certain geographic features in the South China Sea are actually allowed. This approach is not intended to resolve the underlying sovereignty dispute, but rather could help provide greater clarity to existing claims and open the path to other peaceful solutions.

With respect to resolving the claimants' underlying sovereignty disputes, a wide array of mutually agreed third-party dispute settlement mechanisms, including recourse to the International Court of Justice, would be available to them.

Short of actually resolving the disputes, there is another option which past Chinese leaders have called for—namely, a modus vivendi between the parties for an indefinite period or until a more favorable climate for negotiations could be established. In the case of the South China Sea, this could be achieved by any number of mechanisms, including, as a first step, a detailed and binding meaningful ASEAN–China Code of Conduct.

But for any claimant to advance its claims through the threat or use of force or by other forms of coercion is patently unacceptable.

In my testimony before the House Foreign Affairs Subcommittee on Asia and the Pacific in February 2014, I noted U.S. concern over an apparent pattern of behavior by China to assert its nine-dash line claim in the South China Sea, despite the objections of its neighbors and the lack of clarity of the claim itself. More than a year later, China continues to take actions that are raising tensions and concerns throughout the region about its strategic intentions.

In particular, in the past year and a half China's massive land reclamation on and around formerly tiny features, some of which were under water, has created a number of artificial above-water features. Three of China's land fill areas are larger than the largest naturally formed island in the Spratly Islands. China is constructing facilities on these expanded outposts, including at least one air strip on Fiery Cross reef that looks to be the longest air strip in the Spratlys and capable of accommodating military aircraft. China is also undertaking land reclamation efforts in the Paracel Islands, which it currently occupies.

Under international law it is clear that no amount of dredging or construction will alter or enhance the legal strength of a nation's territorial claims. No matter how much sand you pile on a reef in the South China Sea, you can't manufacture sovereignty.

So my question is this: What does China intend to do with these outposts?

Beijing has offered multiple and sometimes contradictory explanations as to the purpose of expanding these outposts and constructing facilities, including enhancing its ability to provide disaster relief, environmental protection, search and rescue activities, meteorological and other scientific research, as well as other types of assistance to international users of the seas.

It is certainly true that other claimants have added reclaimed land, placed personnel, and conducted analogous civilian and even military activities from contested features. We have consistently called for a freeze on all such activity. But the scale of China's reclamation vastly outstrips that of any other claimant. In little more than a year, China has dredged and now occupies nearly four times the total area of the other five claimants combined.

Far from protecting the environment, reclamation has harmed ecosystems and coral reefs through intensive dredging of the sea bed. Given its military might, China also has the capability to project power from its outposts in a way that other claimants do not. And perhaps most importantly, these activities appear inconsistent with commitments under the 2002 ASEAN China Declaration on the Conduct of Parties in the South China Sea, which calls on all parties to forgo actions that "would complicate or escalate disputes."

More recently, Beijing indicated that it might utilize the islands for military purposes. The Chinese Foreign Ministry stated that the outposts would allow China to "better safeguard national territorial sovereignty and maritime rights and interests" and meet requirements for "military defense." These statements have created unease among neighbors, in light of China's overwhelming military advantage over other claimants and past incidents with other claimants. As the statement last week from the ASEAN Leaders Summit in Malaysia made clear, land reclamation in the South China Sea is eroding trust in the region and threatens to undermine peace, security, and stability in the South China Sea.

Apart from reclamation, the ambiguity and potential breadth of China's nine-dash line maritime claim also fuels anxiety in Southeast Asia. It is important that all claimants clarify their maritime claims on the basis of international law, as reflected in the United Nations Convention on the Law of the Sea. On April 29, Taiwan added its voice to the regional chorus by calling on "countries in the region to respect the principles and spirit of all relevant international law, including the Charter of the United Nations, and the United Nations Convention on the Law of the Sea." The ASEAN claimant states have indicated that their South China Sea maritime claims derive from land features. Beijing, however, has yet to provide the international community with such a clarification of how its claims comport with international law. Removing ambiguity goes a long way to reducing tensions and risks.

Simple common sense dictates that tensions and risks would also be reduced if all claimants commit to halt reclamation activities and negotiate the acceptable uses of reclaimed features as part of a regional Code of Conduct. Talks on a regional Code of Conduct over several years have been inconclusive, but we share the growing view in the region that a binding Code should be completed in time for the 2015 East Asia summit in Malaysia.

Mr. Chairman, let me now turn the question of what the United States is doing to ensure peace and stability in the South China Sea.

The United States can and does play an active role in the South China Sea to defend our national interests and international legal principles. And while it falls to the claimants to resolve their disputes, we will continue to play an active and constructive role. U.S. engagement in regional fora has been crucial in placing the South China Sea and maritime cooperation at the top of the agenda in the region's multilateral forums, and these issues are a major part of bilateral discussions with the relevant countries. By shining a spotlight on problematic behavior, including massive land reclamation, the United States has helped ensure that problematic behavior is exposed and censured, if not stopped.

We also play an important role building regional consensus around rules and acceptable practices with regard to maritime and territorial issues. We defend the use of legal dispute settlement mechanisms that may be available to countries—including arbitration under the Law of the Sea Convention—when diplomatic negotiations have not yielded results.

I would like to make two points regarding the Law of the Sea Convention. First, with respect to arbitration, although China has chosen not to participate in the case brought by the Philippines, the Law of the Sea Convention makes clear that "the absence of a party or failure of a party to defend its case shall not constitute a bar to the proceedings." It is equally clear under the Convention that a decision by the tribunal in the case will be legally binding on both China and the Philippines. The international community expects both the Philippines and China to respect the ruling, regardless of outcome.

Secondly, I respectfully urge the Senate to take up U.S. accession of the Law of the Sea Convention. Accession has been supported by every Republican and Democratic administration since it was transmitted to the Senate in 1994. It is supported by the U.S. military, by industry, environmental groups, and other stakeholders. I speak in the interests of U.S. foreign policy in the South China Sea in requesting Senate action to provide advice and consent to accede to the Convention. Doing so will help safeguard U.S. national security interests and provide additional credibility to U.S. efforts to hold other countries' accountable to their obligations under this vitally important treaty.

Another line of effort is our work to forge strong partnerships with Southeast Asian coastal states to improve their maritime domain awareness so they have a clearer picture of what is developing in waters off their mainland coasts. We are also working with allies such as Japan and Australia to coordinate and maximize the impact of our assistance and to ensure that we are not duplicating efforts. By developing a common operating picture, claimants can work together to avoid unintended escalations and identify potential areas of cooperation.

We have also encouraged the sharing of information and enhanced coordination amongst the claimants and others in the region to ensure that all countries with an interest in the peaceful resolution of disputes in the South China Sea are aware of events there, and understand what everyone else is doing.

My colleague Assistant Secretary for Defense, Dave Shear, will speak next about the military implications of recent developments as well as the Department of Defense's efforts to ensure regional peace and stability. It is my belief that the consistent presence of the Seventh Fleet and our recent force posture movements have been significant factors in deterring conflict between claimants in recent years. Disputes in the South China Sea have simmered, but not boiled over.

But against the backdrop of a strong and sustained U.S. military presence, which is welcomed by the overwhelming majority of countries in the region, diplomacy will continue to be our instrument of first resort. We are vigorously engaging with all of the claimants. We do so at major multilateral meetings like the East Asia summit and ASEAN Regional Forum and we do so bilaterally, as President Obama did in Beijing late last year. Next week, I will host my 10 ASEAN counterparts here in Washington and then will accompany Secretary Kerry to China in advance of the Strategic and Economic Dialogue he will host this summer. In each of these meetings, we will push forward on restraint and push back against destabilizing behavior; we will push for respect for the rules and push back on unilateral actions to change the status quo.

Mr. Chairman, the net effect of what we are seeing in the South China Sea is a heightened interest from the region in ensuring that the existing rules-based order remains intact as well as a strengthened demand for the United States to continue playing a leading role in regional security affairs.

Despite our differences over the South China Sea, the United States and China have worked hard to expand cooperation and develop effective channels of communication to manage differences. This administration has been clear and consistent in welcoming China's peaceful rise, and in encouraging China to take on a greater leadership role in addressing regional and global challenges. This was demonstrated clearly by our two countries' joint announcement of climate targets and military CBMs last November in Beijing. We are working with China constructively on a wide range of security and other challenges—including with respect to North Korea, Iran, climate change, and global healthy security. Moreover, we actively encourage all countries to pursue constructive relations with China, just as we urge China to take actions that reassure the region of its current and future strategic intentions. As President Obama pointed out recently, there is much to admire about China's rise and reason for optimism with regard to cooperation. But as he also noted, we cannot ignore attempts by any country to use its "sheer size and muscle to force countries into subordinate positions," including in the South China Sea. For the President and Secretary of State on down, maritime issues remain at the top of this administration's agenda with Beijing. We consistently raise our concerns directly with China's leadership and urge China to manage and resolve differences with its neighbors peacefully and in accordance with international law. We also underscore that the United States will not hesitate to defend our national security interests and to honor our commitments to allies and partners in the Asia-Pacific.

Fundamentally, these maritime security issues are about rules, not rocks. The question is whether countries work to uphold international legal rules and standards, or whether they flout them. It's about whether countries work together with others to uphold peace and stability, or use coercion and intimidation to secure their interests.

The peaceful management and resolution of disputes in the South China Sea is an issue of immense importance to the United States, the Asia-Pacific region, and the world. This is a key strategic challenge in the region. And I want to reaffirm here today that we will continue to champion respect for international law, freedom of navigation and overflight and other internationally lawful uses of the seas related to those freedoms, unimpeded lawful commerce, and the peaceful resolution of disputes.

Mr. Chairman, I thank you for this opportunity to appear before you today to discuss this important issue. I look forward to answering any questions you may have.

STATEMENT OF THE HON. DAVID B. SHEAR, ASSISTANT SECRETARY OF DEFENSE FOR ASIAN AND PACIFIC SECURITY AFFAIRS, U.S. DEPARTMENT OF DEFENSE, WASHINGTON, DC

Ambassador SHEAR. Thank you very much, Mr. Chairman, Ranking Member Cardin, Senator Gardner. Thank you very much for inviting me to join you all today.

I am particularly pleased to testify alongside my friend and colleague, Assistant Secretary Danny Russel. Danny has already framed the challenges we face in the South and East China Seas, so I will focus my remarks on defense implications and the actions DOD is taking.

It is important to note that the territorial and maritime disputes in the South China Sea, while troubling, are decades old. All the claimants except Brunei have developed outposts in the South China Sea. In the Spratly Islands, Vietnam has 48 outposts, the Philippines eight, China eight, Malaysia five, and Taiwan one. All of these claimants have also engaged in construction activity of different scope and degree.

That said, China's reclamation of 2,000 acres just since early 2014 dwarfs the efforts all of the other claimants, and this suggests new and troubling changes in the regional status quo.

China's land reclamation could potentially have a range of military implications, if China chooses to pursue them. These could include developing long-range radar and ISR aircraft, berthing deeper-draft ships, and developing a divert airfield for carrier-based aircraft. These types of actions could prompt other regional governments to strengthen their own military capabilities at their outposts, increasing the risk of miscalculations, crises, and arms races.

It is important to note, however, that we do not really know at this point how the Chinese intend to use these facilities exactly. China could reduce the strategic uncertainty by halting reclamation activities, entering into discussions with other claimants about establishing limits to military upgrades in the South China Sea, negotiating a code of conduct, and clarifying its claims in accordance with international law.

We have made our views on this crystal clear to the Chinese on multiple occasions at the senior-most levels. Our interests, of course, include peaceful resolution of disputes, freedom of navigation and overflight, unimpeded lawful commerce, respect for international law, and the maintenance of peace and stability.

DOD is taking active steps to ensure that U.S. national interests in the South China Sea are adequately protected.

First, we are modernizing our important alliances, Japan, the Philippines, and Australia. With Japan, we recently concluded the new guidelines on United States-Japan defense cooperation, which will greatly increase the scope of United States-Japan defense cooperation. With the Philippines, last year, we concluded the Enhanced Defense Cooperation Agreement, which will ultimately allow the stationing of rotational United States Forces in the Philippines. And in Australia last year, we concluded the force posture agreement, which will allow the increased stationing of Marines and Air Force in Australia on a rotational basis.

Second, we are adopting a more geographically distributed, operationally resilient, and politically sustainable defense posture throughout the region. For example, our new rotational deployment of Littoral Combat Ships to Singapore is the Navy's first sustained forward presence in Southeast Asia since the closing of our naval base at Subic Bay in the early 1990s.

We are leveraging in-theater assets to enhance our visible presence in the Asia-Pacific. In an average month, we are conducting port calls in and around the entire South China Sea. We are flying regular regional intelligence, surveillance, and reconnaissance missions, or ISR missions. We are conducting presence operations, exercising with allies and partners, and maintaining a persistent surface ship presence through routine transits.

Third, we are helping regional governments improve their maritime security capacity and maritime domain awareness. For example, we have transferred Coast Guard vessels to the Philippines and are helping to build the Philippines national coast watch system. We are providing equipment and infrastructure support to the Vietnamese Coast Guard and are helping to support effective maritime security institutions there. We are also conducting a wide range of training exercises and activities with many allies and partners in Asia.

Fourth, we are seeking to reduce the risk of miscalculation and unintentional conflict with China through healthy but prudent military-to-military engagement. Over the past year, through initiatives like the confidence-building measures our two Presidents agreed to last fall, we have made significant and prudent progress in our bilateral defense relationship.

In conclusion, we share the committee's concerns about China's land reclamation and appreciate this opportunity to give you a sense of our thinking. We are actively assessing the military implications of land reclamation and are committed to taking effective and appropriate action.

In addition to building our own capabilities, we are building closer, more effective partnerships with our allies and partners in the region to promote peace and stability.

Thank you, Senators. I look forward to answering your questions.

[The prepared statement of Ambassador Shear follows:]

PREPARED STATEMENT OF DAVID SHEAR

INTRODUCTION

Thank you very much Chairman Corker. Thank you also to Ranking Member Cardin and the members of the committee for inviting me to speak with you today.

I'm pleased to be here to discuss maritime developments in the Asia-Pacific, including how issues like China's land reclamation in the South China Sea affect U.S. security interests. I'm particularly pleased to testify alongside my long-time colleague and friend, Assistant Secretary Danny Russel.

I'd like to start by saying that this is an important issue and a timely hearing. I certainly share your concerns about recent developments in the East and South China Seas. Before I discuss my views on the problem in more detail, I'd like to lay out some of the context for the recent developments in the region.

EAST CHINA SEA

In the East China Sea, through a persistent military and paramilitary presence as well as the announcement in November 2013 of a new Air Defense Identification Zone, China continues to engage in actions that appear designed to challenge Japan's administration of the Senkaku Islands. As President Obama noted in Tokyo last year and reiterated again last week during Prime Minister Abe's visit, "our treaty commitment to Japan's security is absolute, and article 5 covers all territories under Japan's administration, including the Senkaku Islands"—a point that Secretaries Carter and Kerry also reaffirmed with their Japanese counterparts on Monday, April 27, 2015, during the "2+2" meeting in New York. We have been clear, and remain so, that while we do not take a position on the question of sovereignty, the islands are under the administration of Japan. We will continue to oppose any unilateral action that seeks to undermine Japan's administration.

SOUTH CHINA SEA

The challenges we face in the SCS, while troubling, are not new. In fact, the territorial and maritime disputes are decades old. These disputes are centered around three primary areas: the Paracel Islands, claimed by China Taiwan, and Vietnam; Scarborough Reef, claimed by China, Taiwan, and the Philippines; and the Spratly Islands (which include over 200 features, most of which are underwater) claimed all or in part by Vietnam, the Philippines, China, Malaysia, , and Taiwan. Indonesia's maritime claims also project into the South China Sea.

Over the past two decades, all of the territorial claimants, other than Brunei, have developed outposts in the South China Sea, which they use to project civilian or maritime presence into surrounding waters, assert their sovereignty claims to land features, and monitor the activities of other claimants. In the Spratly islands, Vietnam has 48 outposts; the Philippines, 8; China, 8; Malaysia, 5, and Taiwan, 1. All of these same claimants have also engaged in construction activity of differing scope and degree. The types of outpost upgrades vary across claimants but broadly are comprised of land reclamation, building construction and extension, and defense emplacements. Between 2009 and 2014, Vietnam was the most active claimant in terms of both outpost upgrades and land reclamation, reclaiming approximately 60 acres. All territorial claimants, with the exception of China and Brunei, have also already built airstrips of varying sizes and functionality on disputed features in the Spratlys. These efforts by claimants have resulted in a tit-for-tat dynamic which continues to date.

CHINA'S ACTIVITIES

While other claimants have upgraded their South China Sea outposts over the years, China's land reclamation activity vastly exceeds these other claimants' activities. Since 2014, China has reclaimed 2,000 acres—more land than all other claimants combined over the history of their claims. When combined with a range of activities, including: assertion of its expansive Nine-Dash Line claim, relocation of oil rigs in disputed maritime zones, efforts to restrict access to disputed fishing zones, and efforts to interfere with resupply of the Philippine outpost at Second Thomas Shoal, we see a pattern of behavior that raises concerns that China is trying to assert de facto control over disputed territories, and strengthen its military presence in the South China Sea.

We are concerned that the scope and nature of China's actions have the potential to disrupt regional security. China's actions and increased presence could prompt other regional governments to respond by strengthening their military capabilities at their outposts, which would certainly increase the risk of accidents or miscalculations that could escalate. In contrast to China, the other claimants have been relatively restrained in their construction activities since the signing of the China-ASEAN Declaration of Conduct (DOC) in 2002. This restraint may not hold in the face of China's unprecedented altering of the post-DOC status quo.

Furthermore, China's ultimate intentions regarding what to do with this reclaimed land remain unclear. A Chinese spokesperson said on April 9 that it was carrying out reclamation work to "better perform China's international responsibility and obligation in maritime search and rescue, disaster prevention and mitigation, marine science and research." However, the spokesperson also said China will use this construction to better safeguard "territorial sovereignty and maritime rights and interests . . . (and for) . . . necessary military defense." This is not reassuring.

Militarily speaking, China's land reclamation could enable it, if it chose, to improve its defensive and offensive capabilities, including: through the deployment of long-range radars and ISR aircraft to reclaimed features; ability to berth deeper draft ships at its outposts and thus to expand its law enforcement and naval presence further south into the South China Sea; and, airstrips will provide China with a divert airfield for carrier-based aircraft, enabling China to conduct more sustained air operations. Higher end military upgrades, such as permanent basing of combat aviation regiments or placement of surface-to-air, antiship, and ballistic missile systems on reclaimed features, would rapidly militarize these disputed features in the South China Sea.

To be clear, the United States welcomes China's peaceful rise. We want to see a reduction—not an escalation—of tensions in the South China Sea, we want to see a diplomatic solution to these disputes, and we want constructive relations between China and other claimants. But as the President pointed out on April 9, "(w)here we get concerned with China is where it is not necessarily abiding by international norms and rules, and is using its size and muscle to force countries into subordinate positions." These concerns are amplified when put into the broader context of China's rapidly increasing, and opaque defense budget—a budget that has more than doubled since 2008. As well as China's comprehensive military modernization effort that includes investments in capabilities such as ballistic missiles, antiship cruise missiles, and counterspace weapons. Though increased military capabilities are a natural outcome of growing power, the way China is choosing to advance its territorial and maritime claims is fueling concern in the region about how it would use its military capabilities in the future. Having these capabilities per se is not the issue—the issue is how it will choose to use them.

China's actions are not viewed solely in the context of territorial and maritime disputes; they are viewed as indicators of China's long-term strategic intentions. China's unwillingness to exercise restraint in its actions or transparency in its intentions is deepening divisions between China and its neighbors, as ASEAN leaders expressed collectively at the last ASEAN summit in April. As a result, our allies and partners are seeking to deepen their defense, security and economic relationships with us and with each other. China could reduce strategic uncertainty by taking concrete steps to: clarify or adjust its Nine Dash Line claim in order to bring it into accordance with international law as reflected in the Law of the Sea Convention; to renounce any intent to claim a territorial sea or national airspace around any artificial features formed by China's reclamation activities; halt reclamation activity and enter into discussions with other claimants about establishing limits to military upgrades in the South China Sea (either unilaterally and voluntarily as a confidence-building measure or in coordination with other claimants); and rapidly conclude a binding South China Sea Code of Conduct with ASEAN member states.

CURRENT DOD ACTIVITIES

DOD is taking action to protect U.S. national interests in the South China Sea: peaceful resolution of disputes, freedom of navigation and overflight, and other internationally lawful uses of the sea related to these freedoms, unimpeded lawful commerce, respect for international law, and the maintenance of peace and stability. These objectives are directly linked to the continued prosperity and security of the United States and the Asia-Pacific region. We therefore have a strong interest in how all claimants, including China, address their disputes and whether maritime claims accord with international law.

First, we are committed to deterring coercion and aggression and thereby reinforcing the stability of the Asia-Pacific region, and we are taking proactive steps to do so. Our primary effort in this regard is to work to refresh and modernize our long-standing alliances. With Japan, we concluded last week a historic update to our bilateral Guidelines for U.S.-Japan Defense Cooperation, with an eye to enhancing the ability of the U.S.-Japan Alliance to support peace and security across the region and the globe. With the ROK, we are developing a comprehensive set of Alliance capabilities to counter the growing range of threats on the peninsula, while expanding our ability to tackle global challenges together. And in Australia and the Philippines, we signed ground-breaking agreements in 2014 that will provide enhanced access for U.S. forces while greatly expanding the combined training opportunities for our alliances.

To expand the reach of these alliances, we are embarking on unprecedented "trilateral" cooperation—in other words we are networking our relationships. In some cases this cooperation directly benefits our work on maritime security. For example, we're cooperating trilaterally with Japan and Australia to strengthen maritime security in Southeast Asia and explore defense technology cooperation.

Second, we are adapting our overall defense posture in the region to be more geo-graphically distributed, operationally resilient, and politically sustainable. For example, we're shifting our Marines from a concentrated presence in Okinawa to Australia, Hawaii, Guam, and mainland Japan. We are already leveraging changes in our force posture to make existing engagements more robust. Our rotational deployments of Littoral Combat Ships to Singapore has provided the U.S. Navy with its first sustained forward presence in Southeast Asia since the closing of Subic Bay in the early 1990s and has opened the door for greater training and engagement opportunities with our allies and partners in Southeast Asia.

We are also leveraging the assets we have in theater to maintain and enhance our visible presence in the Asia-Pacific, and the South China Sea. This presence not only reinforces our regional diplomacy, it also deters provocative conduct and reduces the risk of miscalculation in the area. The Department maintains a robust regional presence in and around the South China Sea. In an average month, U.S. military forces are conducting multiple port calls in and around the South China Sea, flying regular regional ISR missions, conducting presence operations, and exer-cising with allies and partners like the Philippines and Malaysia, all while main-taining a persistent surface ship presence with routine transits throughout the area. For example, our new Littoral Combat Ship, the USS *Fort Worth*, recently concluded a successful naval engagement with the Vietnamese Navy that included a full day of at-sea activities. And before her deployment is done, the LCS will have completed bilateral Cooperation Afloat Readiness and Training (CARAT) with seven different Asia-Pacific partners.

Third, we are working with governments in the region to improve their maritime security capacity and maritime domain awareness in order to increase regional transparency and deter further conflict. In the Philippines, for example, we recently concluded the Enhanced Defense Cooperation Agreement and have transferred ves-sels to help our ally police its own waters and are helping to build a National Coast Watch System that will improve Manila's awareness of its maritime domain. The Philippines has also been the largest recipient of U.S. Foreign Military Financing (FMF) funds in the region. These funds have been used to assist the Philippines with communications interoperability, maritime interdiction boats, shipyards capac-ity and patrol vessel upgrades. We are also providing equipment and infrastructure support to the Vietnamese Coast Guard and are helping to support effective mari-time security institutions there. Last October, the U.S. Government took steps to allow for the future transfer of maritime security related defense articles to Viet-nam. We have three annual dialogues with Vietnam on defense cooperation—the Defense Policy Dialogue; Bilateral Defense Dialogue; and Political, Security, and Defense Dialogue.

To support efforts to improve the maritime domain awareness of our allies and partners, we are encouraging greater information sharing in the region. PACOM will be hosting a workshop with our ASEAN partners next month to discuss lessons-learned and best practices in maritime domain awareness, to include information-sharing. We also support initiatives from within the region like the Regional Co-operation Agreement on Combating Piracy and Armed Robbery against Ships in Asia (ReCAAP) Information Sharing Center and Changi Information Fusion Center in Singapore to encourage greater collaboration among our allies and partners to establish a timely and accurate common operating picture of maritime activities in the region.

Furthermore, DOD has a robust slate of training exercises and activities with many allies and partners in Asia, and we have begun incorporating a maritime focus into many of these engagements. Exercise Balikatan, our premier joint exer-cise with our Philippine allies, ended last week and is a great example of a long-standing exercise with a key ally that has evolved to meet new security challenges. This year's Balikatan focused on a territorial defense scenario off the Sulu Sea. This is the largest of more than 400 planned events we have with the Philippines to assist this important ally with a credible defense of its borders and territorial waters. We also conduct regular bilateral naval exercises with the Indonesians, in-cluding Cooperation and Readiness Afloat (CARAT) and Sea Surveillance Exercises (SEASURVEX) that focus on improved interoperability through maritime patrols, surveillance, vessel boarding, fixed and rotary wing naval aviation. The most recent SEASURVEX took place 6–10 April out of Batam, Indonesia, which included a flight portion over the South China Sea.

We're also creating new defense engagements where needed. The Marines, for example, participated in their first amphibious exercise with the Malaysian Armed Forces last year. For the first time, last August, the United States trained with the

Malaysia Armed Forces in Eastern Sabah for MALUS AMPHEX 2014. MALUS AMPHEX 2015 is scheduled for later this summer. We are also conducting routine CARAT exercises with Malaysia with the next scheduled for the summer where, as with Indonesia, we will focus on, among other things, navigation and communications, interoperability and maritime air surveillance.

While the United States is doing a lot to help build partner capacity and regional cooperation on maritime security challenges, we aren't doing it alone. There is broad agreement on the importance of maritime security and maritime domain awareness, and we're working closely with our friends in Australia, Japan, South Korea, and elsewhere to coordinate and amplify our efforts toward promoting stability and prosperity in Asia.

Fourth, we are seeking to reduce the risk of miscalculation and unintentional conflict with China in the South China Sea or elsewhere in Asia. To do so, we continue to speak out against China's disruptive behavior publically and privately. We also continue to call on China to clarify its Nine Dash Line claim under international law. And we will continue to urge all claimants to exercise self-restraint and pursue peaceful and diplomatic approaches to their disputes.

At the same time, we are also working to build transparency and improve understanding with China through mil-to-mil ties. Over the past year, through initiatives like the confidence-building measures our two Presidents agreed to last fall, we have made significant and prudent progress in our bilateral defense relationship. This year, we will be working to complete another measure that aims to prevent dangerous air-to-air encounters. In addition, we have institutionalized several key defense policy dialogues to include the Under Secretary-led Defense Consultative Talks and the Assistant Secretary-led Asia-Pacific Security Dialogue where we discuss a range of regional security issues, including our concerns about the South China Sea. We also hold discussions on operational safety in the maritime domain at the Military Maritime Consultative Agreement Talks.

CONCLUSION

In conclusion, we share the committees' concerns about China's land reclamation and appreciate this opportunity to give you a sense of our thinking. We are deeply engaged with the State Department, the NSC, and other interagency partners in adapting our integrated, whole of government response to meet evolving challenges. We are actively assessing the military implications of land reclamation and are committed to taking effective and appropriate action. In addition to building our own capabilities, we are also building closer, more effective partnerships with our allies and partners in the region to further peace and stability.

The United States is a resident power in the Asia-Pacific. In addition to our significant economic and security interests in the region, we have more than 7,000 miles of Pacific coastline and more than 16 million citizens who trace their ancestry to the Asia-Pacific. Given the importance of the Asia-Pacific to our interests, we owe it to the American people to think, not just about the challenges of today, but also the potential problems of tomorrow. And in this respect, our regional friends and partners should rest assured—we will continue to protect security and promote prosperity of the Asia-Pacific and above all, we will honor our commitments.

The CHAIRMAN Well, thank you, both. I appreciate the testimony. We were preparing for this meeting and our staff, doing the great job they do, came in and had some pretty hot comments for me to make relative to China. And I knew you guys were going to say something very similar to what you just said. I just do not see us doing anything that is real to alter this.

So the comments that both of you made are interesting, involving long-term things that will not immediately stop what is happening.

So I just want to ask a question: How long do we think it will be before what China has done with these islands and others is irreversible? I mean, it is not going to be the many years that you guys just laid out it would take for any longer term effect to have occurred. It is going to be in a very short amount of time.

Would both of you all agree that, on the current pace, the change has already occurred and is going to be almost irreversible? Is that correct?

Mr. RUSSEL. Mr. Chairman, I do not know analysts who believe that the sand that has been dredged and formed into landfill in the South China Sea is going back into the water, but the key question that the administration is focusing on is what will China do, what is China's behavior? And it is China's behavior that we are influencing through the multiple tracks of diplomacy, leveraging our other instruments of power, and, of course, our substantial presence.

The CHAIRMAN I do not see their behavior changing. It seems to me that, in a very short amount of time, they are going to have de facto control of the South China Sea.

I guess I would ask our military leader, what is it that we think that is toward? Do we think they want to claim that as international space for them to have dominion over? What do you think their end is today?

Ambassador SHEAR. Well, at a minimum, Mr. Chairman, I think the Chinese are trying to demonstrate administrative control over those features. They are trying to legitimate their claims to these features.

I would note, however, that on the basis of international law, many of the features the Chinese and other claimants are building on are submerged features that do not generate territorial claims. So it is difficult to see how Chinese behavior, in particular, comports with international law.

With regard to how the Chinese use the reclaimed features, it is our estimate that it will be 2017 to 2018 before the Chinese complete construction of the airfield on Fiery Cross Reef. So it will take some time for them to construct that airfield.

Again, as Assistant Secretary Russel has said, how the Chinese use those facilities is the important question facing us now. We can have an influence on how the Chinese will use those features, and we are in the process of ensuring that the Chinese have a crystal clear view of what we think about their use of those features.

Mr. RUSSEL. Mr. Chairman, if I could interject, the Chinese are already paying a significant price for their behavior in the form of the pushback by the countries in the region against what they are doing.

The Chinese set out three important goals for the South China Sea policy: no criticism, no internationalization of the issue, and what they call no legalization of the issue. And they have failed on all fronts, three strikes.

They are the target of substantial international criticism, including just last month by the 10 ASEAN leaders. This issue is debated and discussed to their consternation in multilateral fora. And the case brought by the Philippines to the U.N. Law of the Sea tribunal, which the Vietnamese themselves have also weighed in on, is arguably legitimate access to international legal mechanisms, the very things that the Chinese sought to avoid.

I think if we want proof that this opprobrium and diplomatic pushback has an effect on the calculus of Beijing's leaders, we can look at the example that Senator Cardin cited, namely the deployment of the oil rig off the coast of Vietnam where, after a face-saving period of a few weeks, the Chinese moved the rig out and subsequently have only sent it to explore in places where they had the permission of the government concerned.

The CHAIRMAN Have we considered helping the other claimants build out their areas? And do you think they would have any desire for that to occur? Or do they feel cowered in this process also?

Mr. RUSSEL. Mr. Chairman, we are helping all the countries, including the claimants, in Southeast Asia to build their capacity to defend their coastal borders.

The CHAIRMAN I am talking about building out their claims in the South China Sea, helping them with that in any way, which would be a more direct way of ensuring that China does not overtake the area. I know it is not something that I have heard discussed, but is that something we considered doing? Something that is very direct, versus these other activities, which seem to me are going to be a day late and a dollar short, based on the current trajectory?

Mr. RUSSEL. Mr. Chairman, we discourage, not encourage, the construction of outposts or the reclamation or the construction of potential military facilities by any claimant on these islands and shoals. So what is good for the goose is good for the gander.

The problem is the scale and scope, as you pointed out, of China's reclamation activities combined with its military capabilities put it in a different category. What we are doing, as Assistant Secretary Shear referenced, is working with allies, including the Philippines, through things like the EDCA Agreement to expand our access and our military presence to ensure that we can continue to maintain the stability that we have had for the previous 6-plus decades.

The CHAIRMAN. With the bilateral relationship that we have with China and the economic interests that we have there, does that stifle us from being a little bit more engaged directly in this issue?

Mr. RUSSEL. Any policymaker weighs all of the factors in making decisions about how to leverage our economic relationships or the other aspects of relationships with a country as large as China. But our strategy is built on the premise that we must push back on problematic behavior and that we must make clear, using all instruments of national power and as a whole-of-government effort, where we object and why we object. And we have made the set of concerns clear to the Chinese at high levels. We have also pointed out the negative effect that Chinese behavior has on not only congressional but broad public and business support for the United States-China relationship.

So I think the short answer is that there are direct costs to China in its economic and political relationship with the United States for provocative or destabilizing behavior. But our goal, Mr. Chairman, is to build a solid, cooperative relationship with China that is consistent with our principles and that is consistent with our national interests.

The CHAIRMAN Thank you very much.

Senator Cardin.

Senator CARDIN. Secretary Russel, I assume that you are referring to the 10 leaders of ASEAN's statement during the recent meeting where they said that China's actions, ''eroded trust and confidence and may undermine peace, security, and stability in the South China Sea.''

Mr. RUSSEL. That is correct.

Senator CARDIN. See, I looked at that as a weak statement, not a strong statement. I was looking for a stronger action by ASEAN. Am I wrong? Were we satisfied with the response?

Mr. RUSSEL. I would say, Senator, that that statement is a 7 on the Richter scale of ASEAN statements. It is a strong statement in the following respect. The Chinese have worked single-mindedly and energetically to discourage, if not deter, the countries of ASEAN from speaking out publicly, and they have worked as well through close friends of theirs within ASEAN to try to prevent the very outcome that they saw.

Given the soft-spoken quality of the Southeast Asians, that is a ringing indictment to China's behavior.

Senator CARDIN. I wish I had you as one of my professors in college grading my papers. I think you are being pretty gentle.

We have been waiting for ASEAN for a long time on this code of conduct, and I understand we have limited ability to control the way that they proceed on this, but can you just give me your observation, whether we can anticipate that they will, in fact, move ahead with a code of conduct that would be considered the gold standard as to how these disputes should be handled, from the point of view of eliminating these provocative type actions that have taken place?

Mr. RUSSEL. First of all, Senator Cardin, we are not waiting for ASEAN. We are working with ASEAN. We are encouraging ASEAN. And we are creating the space and the confidence that allows ASEAN to engage both diplomatically but also politically with China.

I think that the foot-dragging on the code of conduct is a problem, and that is something that we shine a light on and encourage the parties, and particularly China, to get serious about resolving.

But the more fundamental point is that China has already made a commitment; made a commitment to avoid and refrain from provocative actions that complicate these issues or make it more difficult to resolve them in 2002, in the declaration of conduct.

So I think the real issue is not that ASEAN and China have not yet achieved a code of conduct, as much as we wish it, but rather that the parties are not adhering to the spirit and letter of the declaration of conduct.

Senator CARDIN. But I would anticipate that, under a code of conduct, there would be established avenues for resolving disputes other than taking unilateral action, but maybe we are asking for too much. It seems to me that the ASEAN countries have been talking about this for a long time.

And I am not as satisfied as you are on the progress that we have seen to date, and I just hope that they can get their act together to give us some hope.

Secretary Shear, if I might, in your statement, both written and oral, you spoke about our military alignments in the region, the types of deployments and the types of exercises that we have had.

Is this a direct response to additional challenges that could be there because of maritime security concerns? And do we have enough assets and resources to deal with the potential threat in that region?

We do have certain obligations, certain treaty obligations, that the President has underscored. Do we have the facilities or the assets in place to deal with these potential problems?

Ambassador SHEAR. Senator, we are engaged in a long-term effort to bolster our capabilities in the region. We are engaged in a long-term effort to invest in the technologies we will need to maintain military superiority in the region, and we are engaged in an effort to strengthen our alliances and build capacity of our partners.

Just a few examples of the increases in our capabilities in the region include the deployment of Global Hawks and F–35s to Japan. Soon we will be adding to the stock of the V–22s in Japan as well. We will have four Littoral Combat Ships in Singapore by 2020.

I visited one of those the Littoral Combat Ships, the USS *Fort Worth*, in Singapore in January. These are very capable ships. They travel at 50 knots. They have a 15-foot draft. And they will be able to go places where no warship has been able to go in the past in the region, including opening up new ports for naval warship visits throughout the region.

We are deploying high-speed vessels to Singapore and Guam. We are putting a new Virginia class submarine—an additional Virginia class submarine in Guam as well. So we will have no shortage of capabilities and assets throughout the region to back our diplomacy and ensure deterrence and ensure national security.

With regard to our posture in the region, we are also undergoing an important shift in the way we posture our forces. Under the redeployment of long-term—medium- to long-term redeployment of Marines in Okinawa, we will be moving significant numbers of Marines to Hawaii, Guam, and Australia. We will be operating a mix of additional Air Force assets in Australia on a rotational basis, including fighter, bomber, and tanker aircraft. We are looking at further deployments in the Philippines on a rotational basis, once we have implemented the Enhanced Defense Cooperation Agreement.

So we will have a very strong presence, very strong continued posture throughout the region to back our commitments to our allies and work with our partners to continue ensuring peace and stability in the region, as well as back up diplomacy vis-a-vis China on the South China Sea.

Partner capacity-building will continue to be central to our efforts. We believe that among our most important goals is for our partners in the region to be able to pursue their own interests, which they have in common with us, as vigorously as possible. That is the medium- to long-term goal.

And we are implementing that, in particular, with Vietnam, Malaysia. We hope we will grow our cooperative relationship with Indonesia as well.

So we have strong potential in the region with our partners. With regard to capacity, partner capacity-building, we are working to maximize what we do under existing authorities and with existing resources. But, of course, we would welcome added resources for this effort and we would put them to good use.

Senator CARDIN. Thank you, Mr. Chairman.

The CHAIRMAN Senator Gardner.

Senator GARDNER. Thank you, Mr. Chairman, and thank you to the witnesses today.

This is an important hearing as we try to understand intentions in an area of the world where we are trying to grow our opportunity as well.

Mr. Chairman, this is a very interesting conversation. It is clear, though, that the People's Republic of China's destabilizing activities in the East China Sea and South China Sea, including what can only be described as a unilaterally imposed Air Defense Identification Zone in the East China Sea or the inexplicable nine-dash line of sovereignty claims that encompass 90 percent of the South China Sea, are a threat to the stability in the region and create a serious challenge to the United States rebalance policy in the Asia-Pacific.

These activities are contrary to China's own, to their very own past pledges and are possibly violations of international law, as we have said.

These actions also threaten the freedom of navigation and sea lanes that are vital to global commerce, and also create an unstable security environment where unintended escalation and military confrontation in the region becomes likely, with dire consequences for all parties involved.

But as we contemplate policy options to address Beijing's actions, we also need to understand their intentions, questions like: Are these actions a show of force intended to intimidate China's smaller neighbors? Are they intended to deter the United States, especially in the Asia pivot policy? Are they driven by economic considerations?

The United States has been the guarantor of peace and prosperity in the region for generations, and we cannot remain complacent in light of these very serious challenges.

So to Assistant Secretary Russel, in your testimony you stated, under international law, it is clear that no amount of dredging or construction will alter or enhance the legal strength of a nation's territorial claims. No matter how much sand you pile on a reef in the South China Sea, you cannot manufacture sovereignty.

Just a couple questions. Could you clarify the legal basis that China is claiming that it has, just talk about the legal basis for its claims? Are they trying to create facts on the ground in this area, hoping that the international community will eventually just say that it is recognized? And do you see any similarities of China's actions to other territorial disputes in the region around the world?

Mr. RUSSEL. Thank you, Senator Gardner. I appreciate your leadership in the Asia-Pacific Subcommittee, so thank you very much for that.

We have real concerns about the lack of clarity to the Chinese claims and have consistently pushed Beijing to clarify its claims in terms that are consistent with international law, and particularly the Law of the Sea Convention. That is above and beyond our concerns about the actual behavior of China itself.

Now, there are ambiguities in the claims of other claimants in the South China Sea. There are many complicated historical factors at work. But the problem we are all looking at, grappling with, is the fact that, under the Law of the Sea, which, as Chairman

Corker pointed out, China itself has ratified and signed, all sovereignty derives from land features. So for the Chinese to claim that, on the basis of a historical map, they are sovereign over the seas of the South China Sea cannot be squared with the way the international law operates.

The case which the Philippines has brought, and now the Vietnamese are supporting, before the tribunal of the Law of the Sea is looking at that very question, not the underlying sovereignty to any land feature, but the expansive and ambiguous claim to maritime space.

Senator GARDNER. We have the upcoming United States-China strategic and economic dialogue this summer. Does the President plan to personally discuss this issue with President Xi in September?

Mr. RUSSEL. In my experience, and I have been a party to virtually every meeting that senior U.S. Government officials, including the President, have had with President Xi Jinping, there has never been a high-level meeting between the President or the Secretary of State and President Xi in which this issue was not raised. It will be raised, and it is raised not because we take one claimant's side against another, or we are against China. It is raised because the behavior associated with China's operations in the South China Sea is having a destabilizing effect on the region and, therefore, a negative impact on our national security interests.

Senator GARDNER. I do not want to blur the two, but it is also something that will be brought up at the United States-China strategic and economic dialogue in the summer, correct?

Mr. RUSSEL. Well, Senator, it will, but it will be brought up as soon as this Saturday when Secretary Kerry travels to Beijing and meets with his counterparts, and on Sunday when he also meets with President Xi Jinping.

Senator GARDNER. Very good.

A couple of comments you made in your testimony that I wanted to follow up on, and I do not remember, I am sorry, Secretary Shear, if this is something you had said or Secretary Russel had said this, but it is China's behavior we are influencing was the response to one question. It was also said that China is already paying a significant price for their behavior.

So the comment that was made of China's behavior that we are influencing, if I could get an example—and I think the chairman was trying to get at this question as well—if I could get an example of where China has changed behavior as a result of us trying to influence that behavior, that would be great. And then on the significant price, I want to follow up on that.

So if I can get an example of where China's behavior has changed as a result of these actions.

Ambassador SHEAR. Sir, if I could draw from my experience as Ambassador to Vietnam. I was in Hanoi at the time the Chinese deployed the oil rig to the South China Sea in the vicinity of the Paracel Islands. During that time, we coordinated closely with the Vietnamese. Of course, we made our views very strongly known in public in Washington and to the Chinese at the time. And the Senate also passed a resolution condemning the Chinese action.

I think all of that contributed to the early withdrawal of the oil rig. I think you can make a strong case supporting the argument that the Chinese withdrew that rig a month earlier than they originally said they would due in part to strong international attention, strong attention from the United States.

Senator GARDNER. So we have the withdrawal of the oil rig. What other behaviors have we influenced?

Mr. RUSSEL. I would add two points, if I may, Senator, to Dave Shear's observation. One is the lack of follow-through to a number of threats that China has made in the past.

So two examples would be their decision not to follow through on an attempt to implement fishing regulations based on Hainan Island and associated regulations based on the declaration of a military district from Sansha City.

The second is the simple fact that after an ill-advised declaration of an ADIZ in the East China Sea—Air Defense Identification Zone—which the United States, Japan, the Republic of Korea, and others immediately objected to and we have made clear in numerous ways, including through the flight of a B–52, that our military operations are not impeded nor do we recognize that zone. The Chinese have gone quiet on that score and have refrained from doing what many people thought and worried they would do, which is to proceed to declare an air defense zone in the South China Sea as well.

So admittedly, these are dogs that have not barked. I am not saying they will never wake up. But it is, I think, certain to those of us who have worked hard on China for a long time that a firm and unified position can affect and generate restraint in terms of Chinese behavior.

Senator GARDNER. Thank you, Mr. Chairman.

The CHAIRMAN Senator Murphy.

Senator MURPHY. Thank you very much, Mr. Chairman, Ranking Member. Thank you to our panelists.

Over the last couple years, I spent a lot of time in and around Ukraine, as have the chairman and ranking member. It is interesting to me some of the parallels with respect to which Russia's actions in Ukraine look sometimes very much like China's actions in the South and East China Seas.

So I wanted to ask a couple questions about whether I am right to understand some parallels here. Clearly, Russia engaged in provocations in eastern Ukraine, up until this day, that involve a thin veneer of separation between themselves and the separatists slowly moving into eastern Ukraine, little green men who are clearly connected and controlling the separatists, in the same way China is being very careful about what they do.

But as they move forward these white-hulled ships rather than these grey-hulled ships, they are actually exerting some additional control over the territory without militarizing the conflict. It seems to me some of the same activities that the Russians are undertaking.

My first question, though, is about the extent to which China is watching what is happening today in and around Ukraine. A lot of us have worried that a lack of a robust response from the United States and Europe in Ukraine kind of sets this new set of rules in which you can reset your borders or territories that you control through channels other than diplomacy. And Russia clearly has gotten away with that thus far.

Is China watching how the Western response plays out to Russia's aggression in Ukraine? Does our ability to send strong messages to Russian matter in terms of what China does next and what new provocations they may look to?

Mr. RUSSEL. Thank you very much, Senator Murphy.

The first point I would make is that while there are some analogies between the behavior of Russia in Crimea and Ukraine and other problems, including China's behavior, I think it is dangerous if not treacherous to try to overdraw any comparison.

In terms of very significant differences, China is not physically seizing territory possessed by or controlled by another country. They are not evicting people from contested land features. They are not nationalizing territory and so on. So there are some very important distinctions.

But it is, certainly, reasonable to assume that the Chinese watch closely and analyze not only what Russia is doing, but how the United States and the international community respond.

One lesson that has to be crystal clear to China is that the Russians and the Russian economy have paid a devastatingly high price for an ill-considered tactical move. I hope and I believe that that example has a chastening effect as the Chinese leaders make judgments about how they will pursue their claims vis-a-vis their neighbors in the South China Sea.

Senator MURPHY. Another frequent topic of discussion with respect to Ukraine and Russia is the challenge that this kind of aggression presents to article 5 in NATO, the question as to whether and when our obligations are actually triggered should you see separatists break out inside the borders of a NATO country. There is fairly open talk about the definitions in article 5 and at what point the obligations are to be triggered.

Do we have any similar concerns with respect to our treaties with the Philippines or with Japan with respect to some, again, movement of these white-hulled nonmilitary vessels that are engaging in this provocative behavior, which may not look military on its face? Or are we confident that we know exactly where that line ultimately is crossed that would trigger obligations from the United States under those treaties?

Ambassador SHEAR. With regard to our treaty with the Philippines, when President Obama visited Manila last year, he described our commitment to the defense of the Philippines as iron-clad, and we will keep that commitment. I think that the best thing that we can do with the Philippines in the short term, both to strengthen the alliance and to strengthen our deterrence in the South China Sea, is to implement the Enhanced Defense Cooperation Agreement, which will allow, as I mentioned earlier, the stationing of rotational United States forces in the Philippines.

In the longer term, I think it will be important for us to assist the Philippines in building their own capacity to allow them, as I said earlier, to pursue their own interests in the South China Sea as vigorously as possible.

Senator MURPHY. Is that to mean you do not read any ambiguity into the treaty or the potential provocations that would trigger obligations?

Ambassador SHEAR. Well, I think that if Philippine forces came under attack, we would, certainly, confer urgently and intensively with our Philippine ally with a view toward ensuring the safety and security of the Philippines.

Mr. RUSSEL. Senator Murphy, if I could add, I would perhaps take it one step further.

First of all, unlike NATO, we do not have a multilateral defense arrangement in Asia, but we have five very strong, very solid treaty alliances. And I am proud to say that those alliances are in great shape today.

We have ongoing consultations, ongoing dialogues and discussions, with each of our partners through mechanisms such as the U.S.-Japan 2+2 or the strategic security dialogue that Assistant Secretary Shear and I cochaired in Manila just 2 months ago.

There is an ongoing discussion about the security situation, so I would not regard this as an off-on switch. The provision of security, whether we are dealing with grey-hulled or white-hulled vessels, is a collaborative and ongoing partnership.

Senator MURPHY. And I do not think that it is any sign of weakness in an alliance or weakness within the scope of a treaty to admit that there are countries that are playing with security guarantees, that are being very careful not to cross lines, and thus precipitating conversations about different scenarios in which there might be a significant amount of grey as to whether or not these treaties become operative.

Certainly, that is happening in NATO today. There are very open conversations about exactly what would trigger article 5, what would not. I do not think anybody sees any weakness in it.

It sounds like you are doing the same thing. I would just encourage it so that we are not surprised by an action that causes us to meditate for too long on whether or not these treaties require our action.

Mr. RUSSEL. Senator Murphy, we are also working with non-treaty-allied partners like Singapore and with important countries like Vietnam or Malaysia and Indonesia, because the goal of our treaties, but the mission of our policy, is to keep the peace and to maintain security. And we will not let these artificial divisions or thresholds create risk for us.

Senator MURPHY. Thank you, Mr. Chairman.

The CHAIRMAN Senator Perdue.

Senator PERDUE. Thank you, Mr. Chairman.

I agree with the President's rebalancing strategy. It is a dangerous world out there, and I think our future, certainly, the 21st century has been characterized as the century of the Pacific, whereas the 20th century may have been the century of the Atlantic.

Over the last 30 years, since China has really opened up, I have been blessed in my career, especially, to have lived there a couple times in the region. I worked in China a lot over the last 30 years. And I have watched United States engage China.

And I do agree with that engagement policy. I hope we can continue that and use military engagement as well as economic engagement. It is a carrot-and-stick type of approach.

Today, though, over the last 20 or 30 years, as their economy has grown and we have grown in terms of consuming their products, we have helped them develop a current account that is dramatically larger than ours, obviously. We have watched their economy grow such that today we have $18 trillion of debt. China and Japan together are the two largest country holders, second only to our own Federal Reserve.

I am very concerned about our ability to continue to engage in a respectful way with China, given the size of our debt. Admiral Mullen, our past chairman of the Joint Chiefs of Staff, said in 2011 that our own national debt is the greatest threat to our national security.

With regard to Asia, and particularly China, how does that debt situation, the fact that they hold a lot of our debt, and I would ask both of you, both from an economic point of view and a military point of view, what does that to do our ability to deal with them straight up, particularly when we have tactical security issues?

Let me give you an example. It has been characterized that we have these, I think you said five, alliances in the region. One of those is Taiwan.

We have an agreement with Taiwan that says if China invades Taiwan or attacks Taiwan, we have to come to Taiwan's defense and help defend Taiwan against China. But to do that, we have to go to China and borrow the money to go to Taiwan and help defend Taiwan against China.

I just want to know the depth at which our own debt situation is hampering our ability to really engage China in a way that we need to over the next 30 years.

Mr. RUSSEL. Well, thank you very much, Senator Perdue, for the question, and also for your work on the committee, which we very much value.

I had the honor to accompany the Vice President of the United States to China within several weeks of Moody's downgrade of the United States credit rating and was on the receiving end of what could only be described as a condescending expression of concern and sympathy by senior Chinese officials. And I was very proud as an American and as a Foreign Service officer at the vigorous way that the Vice President pushed back directly in those meetings in Beijing.

What he said was that no one has ever won a bet who bet against the United States. He said that the vast majority of bonds and the debt of the United States is held by the American people. And he challenged the Chinese, if they wanted to unload, he would have no trouble finding buyers for them.

I cite that as an example of the certainty I bring to answering the question, no, the deficit, the fact that China holds a significant share, albeit perhaps not as big as the share that Japan holds of United States debt——

Senator PERDUE. They are very close, though. They go one and two, back and forth.

Mr. RUSSEL. But that in no way impedes our ability to make national security decisions vis-a-vis China that are in the best interest of the United States people.

I will take the liberty though, Senator, of telling you two things that do impede our ability to effectively pursue our policy in Asia. One is that uncertainty as to whether the United States will, in fact, succeed in adopting and ratifying the Trans-Pacific Partnership trade agreement.

This is, in my experience, the issue that our Asian interlocutors are most focused on and most concerned about. And in just the last 24 hours, the number of expressions of concern and anxiety I have received from Asian counterparts watching the developments on TPA have convinced me that concluding the TPP agreement in 2015 is the single biggest step that we can take to advance our ability to shape the Asian-Pacific region in the 21st century.

And I will take the further liberty of associating myself with Senator Cardin's earlier comment that it would greatly strengthen our hands if the Senate were to ratify the Law of the Sea Convention. That is used against us to discredit our strong arguments on the South China Sea, and inasmuch as both former President Bush and other Republican and Democratic Presidents have endorsed it, I very much hope that the committee would give that some consideration.

Senator PERDUE. Thank you.

Secretary Shear, I would like to switch gears back. That is the economic side. The military side is that China has really increased their investment in their military, such that they are really moving into—I think this is directionally correct. They will be very soon spending about half of what we spend on our military.

The fact that we have a two-theater strategy, and have had for some 60 years or so, if you just do the math, does that not give you concern that over time that that puts us in jeopardy, in terms of being able to project force in the region and affect behavior on the part of China?

Ambassador SHEAR. Thank you very much, Senator.

Chinese military spending, certainly, has grown considerably over the past few years. I believe last year the Chinese defense budget grew by approximately 9.5 percent to reach the public figure of $135 billion. I think if you included activities such as the purchase of foreign weapon systems in the Chinese defense budget, which they do not include, the defense budget could be as high as $165 billion.

They are using these increases in defense spending to quickly modernize their forces and to quickly grow their forces. And we are seeing the effects of that, not only in the South China Sea, but throughout the region.

Senator PERDUE. I am sorry to interrupt. I only have a few seconds left. Could you talk specifically about the naval fleet and their increased investment in the aggressive shipbuilding program they have underway right now, and the long-term, 10-year impact of that on the balance of power in Asia?

Ambassador SHEAR. Well, Senator, it is clear that the Chinese are devoting considerable resources to shipbuilding. Their ability to build ships in a very short timeframe is very high. I do not have the figures at my fingertips, but I can get you those figures for a record.

But, certainly, their capability in terms of the number of ships, and the capability of the weapon systems on those ships, has increased considerably just over the past few years.

Senator PERDUE. Thank you.

Thank you, Mr. Chairman.

The CHAIRMAN Thank you.

I sit here listening and it brings me back to my opening comments about where we were headed before this meeting. I see no price whatsoever that China is paying for their activities in the South and East China Seas. None.

As a matter of fact, I see the price being us paying a price. We are paying the price. We have our friends coming in constantly worried about where we are, what our commitment levels are, pointing out that our foreign military financing in the region is 1 percent of what it is in the rest of the world. They question whether there really is any kind of pivot or rebalance.

So I actually look at what China is doing right now, and I see them paying no price. I see us getting ready to enter into a 123 agreement knowing they are going to violate it. We see them violating international norms now, on this particular issue.

You say that they are being criticized. Gosh, we all get criticized around here all the time. It does not affect our behavior.

So tell me what price they are paying. I see none. I see us actually paying a price in our esteem in the region. I think that our friends are very concerned about us.

And what I see when I visit the region is they see a dominant China, both economically and militarily, and I see them constantly in a state of almost trepidation as to doing anything that might offend them.

Now, what the Philippines did was interesting, and I support their efforts in that regard. I know we are, as a country.

But explain to me the balance here. I think we are the ones that are paying the price by no one seeing any kind of tangible activity relative to this, and they are actually gaining and paying no price.

Mr. RUSSEL. Mr. Chairman, I respectfully but passionately beg to differ. I think, unquestionably, China is paying a price, and it is a growing price for its behavior.

I cited the strong ASEAN push back, but the net result——

The CHAIRMAN Now, wait a minute, wait a minute. My good friend, Senator Cardin, talked about how feckless that response was. You talked about it as a 7 on the Richter scale. It is a different scale than I am accustomed to.

Tell me something that is tangible. I mean, okay, we see a group of people make a statement. Tell me what tangible price China is paying.

Mr. RUSSEL. Number one, the net effect of China's behavior is to strengthen the pull on United States engagement and presence in the Asia-Pacific region from China's neighbors. So we are increasingly in demand. We are sought out as the security guarantor. That is the opposite of an Asian-centric or Sino-centric policy. We have become an even more trusted partner as a result of this behavior.

As I said before, China has failed in the effort to prevent criticism, to prevent internationalization, and, as they see it, embarrassment or even humiliation by virtue of their behavior being taken up as an issue in international fora.

China vigorously opposed and objected to the Philippines introducing a case in the UNCLOS tribunal. And yet, as a result of their action, other claimants, Vietnam, have also weighed in with friend of the court briefs in opposition.

The President of Indonesia, days before traveling to Beijing, made a public statement in which he asserted unequivocally the nine-dash line has no basis in international law.

Coastal states around the South China Sea are developing their own capabilities, their own capacities. They are coming to the United States, they are going to Japan, they are going to Australia, to develop the wherewithal to monitor and to defend and to protect their territorial waters. They are conducting exercises.

And I come back to the fundamental point. They are inviting the United States in. If the Chinese strategy was to freeze us out, not only is it not working, it has backfired.

We are giving the smaller countries the confidence to push back. We are giving them the capabilities to monitor and defend their own territory and their interests.

But most importantly, Mr. Chairman, we have prevented the situation from boiling over.

The CHAIRMAN I do think they are relying more heavily or asking to be able to rely upon us more heavily. I do not see much in the way of substantive changes that are taking place.

Let me move to defense. There are stories in many of the publications this morning about our activities and potentially piloting a boat within 12 nautical miles of one of these islets. Could you talk to me little bit about the effect of that and the importance of that? And are we actually going to do that?

Ambassador SHEAR. Thank you, Mr. Chairman.

With regard to the specific activities or operations mentioned in the Wall Street Journal article, I regret that I am not at liberty to discuss the details of our operations in an unclassified setting. However——

The CHAIRMAN Well, should I call the authors of the article to find more detail? I mean, it is kind of out there.

Ambassador SHEAR. Sir, in general, the Defense Department——

The CHAIRMAN Let me ask you this. Do you think that us cruising within 12 nautical miles of one of these islets on a one-time basis or periodic basis will have an effect on what China is doing?

Ambassador SHEAR. Many of the features in the Spratlys, including those claimed by China, are submerged features. They do not generate a legal territorial claim. We claim the right of innocent passage in such areas, and we exercise that right regularly, both in the South China Sea and globally. And we are going to continue exercising that right both on the surface of the water and in the air.

The CHAIRMAN Let me just ask back again, let us just assume that the authors of this story were on the right path, or let us just ask a hypothetical. Would us cruising our military vessels within

12 nautical miles of these particular islets, would that have some kind of effect on what China is doing?

Ambassador SHEAR. Sir, I am not in a position to comment on the hypothetical situation. But, in general, the Chinese take close notice of our freedom of navigation operations in the South China Sea. They take very close notice of most of our operations in the South China Sea. And they have an effect both on Chinese operations and on Chinese views of our commitment to the security of the region.

And I think our presence and our posture in the region demonstrates repeatedly the continued strength of our commitment to the region and backs what we say to the Chinese with regard to our concerns about their behavior in the South China Sea.

The CHAIRMAN Senator Cardin.

Senator CARDIN. So let me talk a little bit about the impact of China's decision in 2013 to establish the Air Defense Identification Zone in the East China Sea. When that was done, there was a lot of concern. And then it looked like there was just about pragmatic acceptance, not acknowledging legitimacy, but not challenging the activities of flights over that zone.

Can you just give me an update as to the status of flights in that zone, what is being done, and if there is a concern that China may make a similar declaration in the South China Sea?

Mr. RUSSEL. Yes, Senator Cardin.

The President and Vice President and senior officials made clear almost instantly after China's unilateral claim to have created an ADIZ in the East China Sea that we do not recognize it, and we will not accept or abide by it. Other countries, including Japan and the Republic of Korea, that were directly affected, made a similar response.

As a matter of safety and pragmatism, civilian aircraft may choose to circumvent that area, so as to err on the side of safety on behalf of their passengers. But for any aircraft directed by the U.S. Government, any government aircraft, and I will let my colleagues speak to the military aircraft, we do not recognize, we do not accept, we do not avoid that ADIZ.

Now, obviously, not speaking for the Chinese, but it is obvious that they have heard loud and clear the degree to which their neighbors would respond negatively and would oppose the creation of an ADIZ in the South China Sea. And I recognize and commend that restraint.

Senator CARDIN. Just so I have it clear, commercial flights that fly in that area are not complying with the Chinese requirements?

Mr. RUSSEL. The decision about whether or not to enter——

Senator CARDIN. And if they——

Mr. RUSSE [continuing]. Or to respond to a signal from any air traffic controller, regardless of——

Senator CARDIN. But what is happening? Are they responding or not responding? Do we know?

Mr. RUSSEL. I believe that any commercial pilot who takes his passenger plane through an area and, in this case, the specific area in the East China Sea, will respond to queries.

Senator CARDIN. That is what I thought they were doing, so in reality then, China is accomplishing its mission by what it did because they are, in fact, establishing a claim that is not legitimate but making it legitimate by time?

I understood you bristled a little bit at Senator Murphy's comparison between Russia and Ukraine. And I understand the differences, believe me. But I must tell you, when I was over in Asia, the Ukraine was mentioned frequently and concerns about China's unilateral actions were mentioned in the same paragraph.

So if there is a de facto recognition of these zones as being effective in responding to the radio tower, because of the safety of the passengers, I fully understand that.

Is that not an extremely dangerous precedent?

Mr. RUSSEL. It is a precedent that we, certainly, do not want to see repeated, which is why we have made it very clear to the Chinese that we would have great concern with, and object to, any move to declare additional ADIZs in contested areas.

But the decision by a commercial aircraft pilot to respond to a query from a tower in whatever language from whatever base has no bearing on China's claim to sovereignty. Now, it may well be that the Chinese themselves hope to erode the administrative control that Japan exercises in the Senkakus, but that is something that we not only do not support but actively oppose.

Senator CARDIN. And do we believe there is any intention of China to do a similar zone in the South China Sea?

Mr. RUSSEL. It is a topic that I myself have raised with Chinese interlocutors. And while they are not showing their cards, we are. Our cards are unambiguous. It would be a destabilizing and problematic act were China to move in that direction.

Senator CARDIN. Well, I appreciate that, and I agree with that statement. The question is, if they do it, do we have options? What are our options?

Mr. RUSSEL. Senator, of course, we have options, and we are in the business of generating answers to questions about contingencies within the interagency for consideration by the President and his national security team. But I do not see any evidence that we are close to that point.

Senator CARDIN. And I understand we do not want to show all our cards. I understand that we want to be able to reserve the rights to choose our response, based upon what China may or may not do. But it does seem to me that this committee is concerned that there are a lot of risk factors in the China seas—we have a lot of military obligations in the China seas and it will be extremely challenging to protect these alliances, and demanding on the United States. So it would be good to share with us in an appropriate setting how we can be more aggressive in our options to maintain stability and maritime security, and to make clear that provocative actions will not be ignored by us, because it seems to me, yes, we have had strong statements, and I know our actions are limited, but it seems like we are letting certain things go unchallenged which could lead to other provocative actions, which could lead to military conflict, which is something we all want to avoid.

Mr. RUSSEL. Senator Cardin, if I could, very briefly, I have one heartfelt plea: Do not give up on diplomacy. Do not underestimate the power——

Senator CARDIN. This is the committee of diplomacy. We will not give up on diplomacy. We are not the Armed Services Committee. We are the Foreign Relations Committee. We will not give up on diplomacy.

But share with us at times in an appropriate setting what your strategy is in this regard, because at times we think we are not really showing any response to these type of provocative actions, other than issuing a press release. I think we would like to do more, and we would like to have our allies know that we are very much on their side when it comes to these provocative actions.

The CHAIRMAN Senator Gardner.

Senator GARDNER. Thank you, Mr. Chairman.

Just to follow up on Senator Cardin's comments, in response to the question of has China's behavior changed or been influenced by our actions, we cited the oil rig moved out a month ahead when they said it was going to, a lack of follow-through with a threat on some fishing territories, and the Air Defense Identification Zone.

Those seem to be the only three that we talked about. Maybe there are others. But I guess to follow up on Senator Cardin's comments, is there a lack of legislative authority that we need to be discussing here in terms of actions the administration can take through diplomacy, or other areas where we need to be concentrating to show results here?

If their activities, at least on the one island, are completing and 2017 or 2018, we do not have too much time to sit around before completion, if they are going to be serious about claiming that area as some kind of zone or territory.

And the other question I had, is there political cover that the administration is lacking or looking for? Let us have those discussions in ways that we can help to make sure we are providing diplomatic solutions.

Secretary Russel, you talked about the TPP. One concern I had after yesterday's vote—we had the failed cloture vote; hopefully, there are some breakthroughs today that we will move forward on. When we failed to proceed to what is a significant, I believe, opportunity to move forward on TPA, do you think China looks at that? Do they look at that and find I guess new energy, in terms of their efforts to look at the United States as weak or not committed to the region?

Mr. RUSSEL. Thank you, Senator.

To your first question, I mentioned two very specific things, TPP and UNCLOS. I think that we have the full bipartisan support of the Congress behind the strategy of engagement and rebalance. That is valued and tremendously valuable. I think also that the support for the strong United States commitment to rule of law and building a rules-based Asia-Pacific, including with China, is well-recognized and appreciated in the region.

With regard to TPP, China is not the only country that is watching with very intense interest to ascertain whether, to put it colloquially, we can get our act together. And were China or other Asian partners to come to the conclusion over time that the United States will not ultimately be able to follow through and to ratify a TPP agreement that not only sets tremendously high standards in terms of trade investment, environment, labor, governance, et cetera, but more fundamentally creates options for Asian partners, creates the ability to diversify economies so as not to be exclusively dependent on one major commercial partner. Were they to reach that conclusion, our strategic advantages in the Asia-Pacific region would suffer a major setback, I believe.

Fortunately, based on what I know about the TPP agreement, and because it is an agreement that does so much to create jobs and growth in the United States, as well as to create a system of rules that coincide with our vision of an Asia-Pacific in the future, I am convinced that as more and more Members of Congress read the agreement itself, support in the U.S. Congress for the agreement will expand.

Senator GARDNER. My concern, again, just continues to be around whether or not China is able to use the rejection of cloture yesterday to even advance the TPA portion, the Trade Promotion Authority portion, of our trade objectives moving to TPP, that they will use it throughout the region to say the United States is not serious, it is not committed, and try to weaken our relationships amongst the region. That continues to be a concern of mine.

Would it make sense, and perhaps this is best directed to Secretary Shear, would it make sense to have some kind of international maritime operations center as some have suggested in the region to address concerns with territorial issues or claims in the South China Sea?

Ambassador SHEAR. Thank you, Senator.

I would just like to take a moment at the start of my answer to address the issue of Trans-Pacific Partnership.

Secretary of Defense Carter has spoken out energetically in favor of the Trans-Pacific Partnership, because, as Assistant Secretary Russel suggested, he believes it is of great strategic importance to the United States. It does not just provide economic benefits, prospective economic benefits to us, but will bolster our security because it will allow our trading partners to diversify their trading partnerships to the maximum extent possible, and help bind our partners more closely to the United States, not just in economic terms, but in general terms as well.

So, Secretary of Defense Carter strongly supports TPP, because he understands the strategic importance to the United States, the importance of this agreement to U.S. security.

With regard to your second question on the establishment of a regional maritime center, we support efforts like that. As you may know, Singapore has established a data fusion center, which takes information on the situation in the seas around Singapore in the South China Sea and the Indian Ocean and the Malacca Strait and fuses them into a single common picture.

We think our partners throughout the region would benefit greatly by having a common maritime and air picture of the region, so that everybody can view what is going on in the region with complete transparency and calculate their interests accordingly.

With that in mind, the Pacific Command this month is conducting a seminar with like-minded partners from Southeast Asia, ASEAN members and ASEAN claimants, to look at best practices in maritime domain awareness, to look at partner shortfalls in maritime domain awareness. And the results of that seminar will feed into our efforts to strengthen our partners' capacity throughout the region.

Senator GARDNER. And I guess, Secretary Shear, just to follow up, if we support the efforts of some kind of international an operations center, what steps are we doing to make that happen?

Ambassador SHEAR. Well, first of all, we are supporting Singapore in its efforts to broaden the use of its data fusion center. Secondly, with the Philippines, specifically, we support the establishment and operation of their national coast watch center.

So it is not only important for countries to work together to increase their maritime domain awareness, but we are working with individual countries to ensure that they have a good picture of what is going on in the region.

Senator GARDNER. But then are we doing anything on the international operations center itself? And if so, what?

Ambassador SHEAR. I think we could support an international operations center in the region, and we would be happy to explore that with our partners, and we will keep you informed.

Senator GARDNER. But we have not explored that with our partners?

Ambassador SHEAR. We will take the question, sir, and get back to you.

Mr. RUSSEL. If I may just add, in the context of our cooperative work in multilateral fora with ASEAN, including the ASEAN regional forum and the East Asia summit, we have a number of programs and joint exercises that promote collective maritime operations, disaster relief, humanitarian assistance, information-sharing. And promoting both on a bilateral and multilateral basis maritime information-sharing has been a high priority for U.S. programs in ASEAN for the last several years.

Senator GARDNER. So I guess, Secretary Russel, Secretary Shear had said that an international operations center might be something that would be supported. You talked a little bit about the work, the cooperation between the organizations. Is that something we can come to on an international basis with states and others to actually compose one single operation center? Would that be helpful?

Mr. RUSSEL. We will have to take a look at that, but we will gladly do so.

The CHAIRMAN Thank you, Senator.

We appreciate you coming today. I just want to recap, if I could.

Senator Murphy, I think, made some interesting comments, especially having come from Senator Murphy. This committee, as Senator Cardin rightly said, is a committee that focuses on diplomacy. And, Secretary Russel, I know you referred to that, and not giving up on it.

But typically, diplomacy works when people pay a price if it does not. I think the pattern began in August 2013 most clearly to me, August and September 2013, when there was very specific, targeted surgical price for Syria to pay for crossing the redline with chemical weapons. It did not happen.

This committee, along those same timeframes and even before, right after that, passed legislation to cause us to do some things with the Syrian opposition that did not happen, that would have raised the price for Assad.

Then Senator Murphy rightly pointed out the situation with Russia and eastern Ukraine and Crimea. And again, not only this committee, but the Senate unanimously passed a bill raising the stakes so that on the ground Russia would pay a price. Not much of that happened, a very small amount of that, even though it was authorized. The administration did not follow through.

So in the South and East China Seas, I do not think the options are nearly as clear. They are much more vague. And some of the situations there are, certainly, more vague.

But I will say diplomacy only works when people think there is a real price to pay. I do not see any price being paid at all.

I do hope that Secretary Shear will arrange a meeting where he can talk to us clearly about what the U.S. military is getting ready to do, or not getting ready to do. If these reports in the paper this morning are not accurate, then come tell us they are not accurate.

But I would hope that very quickly you would arrange a meeting where Senator Cardin and myself and others can understand what is actually happening here, whether it is just a show or whether something significant is getting ready to occur.

But look, I do not think the decisions around China are easy ones. I think they have learned a lot from us, learned a lot from our own foreign policy over the last 2 or 3 years. And I think this new leadership in China understands that well and understands the things that we are undertaking are interesting, but there is no real price to pay.

So I do not think much is going to change. I get a little worried, even though I think both of you, I know, represent our country well, when we make these statements in these hearings, it just again builds on the narrative that there is a lot of talk coming out of the administration, with not much follow-through. And I do hope that somehow we will develop a coherent policy relative to China that somehow, while they violate international norms in multiple ways, we can figure out a way for a price to be paid.

I do understand that China could be one of those and hopefully is going to be one of those countries where a strong relationship with them is going to benefit not only their citizens but obviously the ones we care about most, our own. I understand all of those things come into play.

But I think you should leave here today with a sense of disappointment from both sides of the aisle about us not really having, still, a coherent policy. The reason this hearing is taking place today is, a year ago, we were concerned about the fact that the United States does not have a coherent policy relative to these issues and others with China. I agree that TPP could be very important. Hopefully, China will accede to TPP over time, if we are able to cause it to come to fruition.

But I leave here as disappointed as I was a year ago about the fact that we do not have a policy. That is certainly not a disappointment in the service that the two of you have provided. We thank you for being here.

The record will remain open through the close of business Friday. Hopefully, if you have questions, you will respond to them quickly.

The CHAIRMAN And without objection, Mr. Ranking Member, the committee is adjourned.

[Whereupon, at 3:52 p.m., the hearing was adjourned.]

ADDITIONAL MATERIAL SUBMITTED FOR THE RECORD

RESPONSES OF DANIEL RUSSEL TO QUESTIONS
SUBMITTED BY SENATOR DAVID PERDUE

Question. President Obama has warned that if TPP is not approved, then "China, the 800-pound gorilla in Asia will create its own set of rules." Can you detail the strategic consequences for the United States if TPP is not approved, and China creates "its own set of rules?"

Answer. Concluding the Trans-Pacific Partnership (TPP) is the most important step we can take in the Asia-Pacific this year, both strategically and economically. We say TPP will be a 21st-century agreement, and we mean it. TPP will certainly address traditional trade issues such as tariffs, market access, and investment. But TPP also gives us the opportunity to protect workers and the environment with the highest and most enforceable standards of any trade agreement ever. And it will allow us to tackle a number of issues that have never been addressed in trade pacts— for instance, it will put disciplines on state-owned enterprises and help en- sure a free and open Internet.

That's why TPP is not just an important trade agreement for the Asia-Pacific region. TPP is an important environmental agreement. TPP is an important labor agreement. TPP is an important transparency and anticorruption agreement.

As President Obama has repeatedly noted, if we cede leadership, if we do not set the rules of the road, our competitors surely will. If we don't lead through TPP, who will maintain a free and open Internet or promote innovation by protecting the intellectual property that innovators have developed? How will companies be protected from unfair competition by state owned enterprises? Where will the protections and enforcement of workers' rights or environmental interests come from?

Question. Do you think it is likely that China would ever be included in the TPP?

Answer. TPP remains open to any country willing to meet its high standards. However, the current focus remains on completing the agreement. TPP is not designed to contain any particular country. Rather it is intended to strengthen and expand the open, transparent, and rules-based system that has been the foundation of the region's peace, stability, development, and prosperity.

Question. Mr. Shear, Mr. Russel, can you expand on the Secretary's remarks regarding the strategic importance and security benefits of approving the Trans-Pacific Partnership?

Answer. Our credibility and our ability to lead are at stake. Countries in the region look to us to help establish the rules and set high standards. While the region seeks greater United States economic engagement, the steady loss of United States trade market share in recent years to Asian competitors, particularly China, feeds an inaccurate perception of United States economic decline. Put more bluntly, the region still welcomes U.S. leadership, but it also still worries about our economic staying power. Failure to complete and approve TPP this year would be a setback to confidence in the United States.

Beyond what we're doing is how we do it, and how this reflects who we are. In today's global economy, the true wealth of a nation lies not in its territory or simple industrial output, but in its ability to maximize its human resources—to help its people to reach their full creative and innovative potential. The United States steady, sustained commitments and engagement over many decades, and our hard work to build fair, inclusive rules that lead to shared growth and opportunity, may not be flashy, but they have helped maintain peace, lift hundreds of millions of people out of poverty, and protect our national interests.

Despite the strengths of the "American brand," we cannot assume that other countries will adopt our free, open economic model and our values. The major question facing both the United States and the region is where do we go from here? I believe the United States and the other economies of the Asia-Pacific will continue to grow and prosper together. That's the future we can build together. But it depends on wise leadership that reinforces our values. Our work supports security and prosperity, which are inherently linked and inseparable.

Question. How will this free trade agreement help us "deepen our alliances" and "promote a global order that reflects both our interests and our values"?

Answer. The United States prosperity and Asia's prosperity are inseparable. We are all aware of the region's spectacular growth in recent decades, and analysts predict significant growth for years to come. The region is home to both the world's two largest economies, excepting the United States, and has many of the world's fastest growing economies as well. The UNDP estimates that the Asia-Pacific will be home to two thirds of the global middle class by the year 2030, and the OECD predicts the region's middle-class consumers will number 2.7 billion by then.

Access to U.S. markets and investment has been crucial for the region's economic growth and development. Bilateral trade in goods and services is now at an all-time high, and U.S. business remains the region's largest source of foreign direct investment, with over $620 billion in investment stock in the region reported in 2013.

For this growth to continue, concluding the Trans-Pacific Partnership (TPP) negotiations, remains the single most important thing the United States can accomplish in its economic and strategic relationship with the Asia-Pacific region this year. There's an urgent question of which future will define East Asia and the Pacific for the century to come. Will the Asia-Pacific reaffirm, strengthen, and expand the open, transparent, and rules-based system that has been the foundation of the region's peace, stability, development, and prosperity? Or will it instead engage in a near-sighted race to the bottom, with arrangements that do not promote shared and sustainable economic growth?

Question. How does China's holding of our debt impact our decisionmaking with regard to security? Particularly with security decisions in this increasingly volatile region?

Answer. China's holding of United States debt does not influence our security decisions. China holds U.S. Treasury securities for the same reason that other investors do—for their safety, and because the market for Treasuries is deep, liquid, and not influenced by individual decisions to buy or sell.

Approximately externally owned U.S. debt is held by a diverse group of countries, and we are not overly reliant on any one overseas holder of U.S. Treasury securities.

While China has a strong interest in the stability of our debt, as a creditor, China's holdings of Treasury securities have no effect on any United States foreign policy decisions.

Question. China last year created the Asia Infrastructure Investment Bank to, "promote interconnectivity and integration in the region." It is clear that Asia has yawning gaps in infrastructure financing that must be addressed. Roads, bridges, ports, railroads, and airports will be key to spurring economic growth in the region. It has been widely reported that the U.S. lobbied other nations not to join the AIIB. However, the United Kingdom, Germany, France, and other Western nations have joined the AIIB.

♦ Can you explain to me why the United States chose not to sign up as a founding member? Do you believe the United States should join the AIIB now?

Answer. As the President has said, we have not and do not oppose the Asian Infrastructure Investment Bank (AIIB), and we are not opposed to other countries participating. We hope the AIIB will operate with robust standards and safeguards and will help borrowers develop sustainable infrastructure in their countries. Moreover, we encourage the ADB and the World Bank to work with the AIIB on a wide range of issues. As for the United States, at present, we are focusing on meeting our commitments to the existing multilateral development banks.

Question. China is currently the United States third-largest export market and biggest source of imports, making it the second-largest overall U.S. trading partner. In 2014, U.S. exports to, and imports from, China were an estimated $125 billion and $466 billion, respectively. According to the U.S. Bureau of Economic Analysis, cumulative Chinese foreign direct investment (FDI) in the United States by the end of 2013 was $8.1 billion, while cumulative U.S. FDI in China was $61.5 billion. At an estimated $341 billion in 2014, the U.S. trade deficit with China is significantly larger than its trade deficit with any other partner. I think that one problem we face now, is that we have gotten out of balance on the trade front with China. I am concerned that this lack of balance on trade is causing China to act out more aggressively.

♦I am curious to get your views, on the economic diplomacy here, if you think that increased trade and economic dependency between our two nations might ease China's recent military behavior?

Answer. Through increased economic ties, we integrate China into the existing rules-based system of trade and make it a more responsive stakeholder in the international system as a whole. This is a process. As time goes on, China may be more likely to change its military posture on the basis of its economic interests. However, there are a number of countries with which China is engaged in strategic competition with whom they share close economic ties. There are also a number of countries which depend on strategic ties with China, but due to a lack of a developed market, do not enjoy a robust economic or trade relationship.

Question. In his address to Congress, Prime Minister Abe told us that Japan is, "resolved to take yet more responsibility for the peace and stability in the world."

During his press conference with the Premier, President Obama reiterated, "our treaty commitment to Japan's security is absolute, and that Article 5 covers all territories under Japan's administration, including the Senkaku Islands . . . and the United States and Japan are united in our commitment to freedom of navigation, respect for international law, and the peaceful resolution of disputes without coercion."

♦(a) Mr. Shear, Mr. Russel, can you detail how the new security guidelines would affect a U.S.-Japanese response to Chinese encroachment against the Senkaku islands?

♦(b) In addition to the new guidelines, Japan has reinterpreted its Constitution to allow a right to collective self-defense. Can you describe Japan's goals in this ongoing reevaluation of its global role?

Answer (a). As reflected in the President's statement quoted above, the United States position on the Senkakus is long-standing: we do not take a position on the question of ultimate sovereignty, but we acknowledge that Japan administers the Senkaku Islands and has done so since the 1972 reversion of Okinawa to Japan. As such, the islands fall under Article V of the U.S.-Japan Treaty of Mutual Cooperation and Security. Article V provides that "[e]ach Party recognizes that an armed attack against either Party in the territories under the administration of Japan would be dangerous to its own peace and safety and declares that it would act to meet the common danger in accordance with its constitutional provisions and processes."

Answer (b). We welcome the Government of Japan's new policy regarding collective self-defense and related security activities. The U.S.-Japan Alliance is one of our most important security partnerships, and therefore we value efforts by Japan to strengthen our bilateral cooperation. In addition, we welcome Japan's goal of playing a greater international role in promoting peace and security, as seen in decisions to send reconstruction and support forces to Iraq and Kuwait, deploy peacekeepers to South Sudan and Haiti, conduct refueling activities in the Indian Ocean, and dispatch Naval assets to counter piracy. We appreciate Japan's efforts to maintain openness and transparency throughout the implementation of this new policy. Japan wishes to build on its contributions to regional and global security, having demonstrated over the last 70 years an abiding commitment to peace, democracy, and the rule of law.

Question. China's Military Modernization.—China recently announced that its defense budget would grow another 10 percent in 2015.

Although official statistics are not reliable, a leading estimate suggests that Chinese defense spending sped past $200 billion per year in 2014, a sixfold increase over the course of 15 years.

Meanwhile, the Pentagon's base budget has fallen by 14 percent over the past 5 years, and the 2015 Department of Defense report on military and security developments involving the People's Republic of China finds that "China's military modernization has the potential to reduce core U.S. military technological advantages."

♦(a) Mr. Shear, Mr. Russel, in light of these facts, do you agree that the regional balance of power continues to shift in China's favor?

♦(b) Has it already reached a point where China has a military advantage over the United States in regional waters, inside the "first island chain"?

♦(c) Is it possible to begin shifting the balance back in our favor while sequestration remains in place?

♦(d) Does the continuing shift in China's favor undermine the U.S. ability to deter provocative behavior, such as China's intimidation tactics in the South and East China Seas?

Answer. The Answer to this question is not within the purview of the Department of State. The Department of State defers to the Department of Defense.

Question. In the 2015 posture statement for U.S. Pacific Command, Admiral Locklear chronicled China's extensive military modernization programs.

It is pursuing an "aggressive ship-building program to produce and field advanced frigates, destroyers, and the first in-class cruiser-sized warship," and will soon begin construction of its first indigenously produced aircraft carrier.

   ♦(a) Mr. Shear, can you summarize what capabilities these new platforms will have in comparison to the U.S. Navy, and those of our regional allies?
   ♦(b) To what extent will China's new naval capabilities facilitate its efforts to enforce its claims in the South and East China Seas?

Answer. The Answer to this question is not within the purview of the Department of State. The Department of State defers to the Department of Defense.

Question. How are America's regional partners and allies responding to the quantitative and qualitative growth in China's military?

Answer. Across the region, we are strengthening our alliances and security partnerships with many countries, who increasingly are asking us for closer security cooperation. Our shared capabilities help us provide additional security to address a variety of traditional and nontraditional challenges. These challenges include, but are not limited to, increasing maritime domain awareness and capacity in light of China's approach to maritime and territorial disputes.

Question. China's participation in RIMPAC.—Some U.S. lawmakers and military leaders have expressed their hope that the administration would cancel China's invitation to attend next year's RIMPAC military exercises.

   ♦(a) Mr. Shear, in light of China's continued regional aggression, can you explain why China should be invited to participate in next year's exercise?
   ♦(b) What does the fact that China sent an intelligence vessel to monitor the 2014 RIMPAC exercises when it was invited to participate in them say about China's distrust of its neighbors and the United States?

Answer. The Answer to this question is not within the purview of the Department of State. The Department of State defers to the Department of Defense.

———

RESPONSES OF DAVID SHEAR TO QUESTIONS
SUBMITTED BY SENATOR DAVID PERDUE

TRADE PROMOTION AUTHORITY/TRANS-PACIFIC PARTNERSHIP

As you know, we are set to vote on Trade Promotion Authority here in the Senate in the near future, which will help the administration finalize the Trans-Pacific Partnership (TPP). In a speech on April 6, Secretary of Defense Ashton Carter said "passing TPP is as important to me as another aircraft carrier. It would deepen our alliances and partnerships abroad and underscore our lasting commitment to the Asia-Pacific. And it would help us promote a global order that reflects both our interests and our values." While we are talking about TPP here, China is finding other ways to gain global influence. China recently started the Asian Infrastructure Investment Bank, and has brought key American allies (including South Korea, Germany, and Britain) on board. At the same time, China is setting up other trade pacts around the region. And, they have been pushing for a pact known as the Free Trade Area of the Asia Pacific. I am concerned about these trade agreements whose rules China can write by virtue of the huge size of its market—China has an official GDP of $10.36 trillion and PPP GDP of $17.63 trillion.

Question (a). President Obama has warned that if TPP is not approved, then "China, the 800-pound gorilla in Asia will create its own set of rules." Can you detail the strategic consequences for the United States if TPP is not approved, and China creates "its own set of rules?"

Answer. As Secretaries Carter and Kerry recently stated, "our strength abroad ultimately rests on the foundation of our vibrant, unmatched, and growing domestic economy." The rules-based system that has brought prosperity to the Asia-Pacific region, and the United States, for many years is now at risk. If the United States does not take the lead in protecting a rules-based approach, we risk ceding leadership to other countries that do not share our interests and our values and are pushing their own regional initiatives with weaker standards. Right now, China and others are negotiating their own agreements. They do not protect workers' rights or environmental interests. They do not protect intellectual property rights or maintain a free and open Internet. And they do not do anything about unfair competition from State-owned enterprises. If that becomes the model for the fastest growing region of the world, it will not only put our workers and firms at a significant disadvantage, it will result in Asian markets being carved up, removing the United States from supply chains, decreasing our linkages to important allies and partners, and seeing our overall influence diminished.

Question (b). Do you think it is likely that China would ever be included in the TPP?

Answer. I refer to the Department of State on this question.

Question (c). Mr. Shear, Mr. Russel, can you expand on the Secretary's remarks regarding the strategic importance and security benefits of approving the Trans-Pacific Partnership?

Answer. As Secretary Carter has said, our military strength ultimately rests on the foundation of a vibrant and growing economy. TPP and the Transatlantic Trade and Investment Partnership (TTIP) would boost our economy and provide our workers and businesses a more fair and level playing field abroad. They also make strategic sense for our country. The agreements would help us promote stability and security in critical regions of the world by deepening our alliances and partnerships abroad, reinforcing U.S. global leadership and engagement, and promoting a global order that reflects both our interests and our values.

Question (d). How will this free trade agreement help us "deepen our alliances" and "promote a global order that reflects both our interests and our values?"

Answer. TPP would cement the strong alliance framework and partnerships that ensure the Asia-Pacific region's security and prosperity. It would greatly increase our cooperation and commercial ties with Japan, Vietnam, Malaysia, and Australia, among others. It would also assure our allies and partners that our long-term commitment to the region reaches beyond security and into the economic realm. Furthermore, concluding the TPP, with countries representing more than 40 percent of global gross domestic product (GDP), would build a magnetic effect attracting non-members across the region to the benefits that it offers.

TPP would also define the values that we want to see prevail in the Asia-Pacific region—values like fair labor standards, environmental protection, and laws updating intellectual property rights. If we can finalize TPP, we will unite the countries representing two-thirds of the world's trade into a coalition of free and fair trade that will drive the standards and rules for the 21st century—a coalition too large for countries to ignore the basic rules that we have agreed on.

CHINESE HOLDING OF U.S. DEBT

Question. In 2014, China was the United States second-largest trading partner, its third-largest export market, its biggest source of imports, and one of the two largest foreign holders of U.S. debt in the form of U.S. treasury securities. Japan has recently passed China as the largest holder of U.S. debt. China has recently seen slowing growth which has caused them to invest more of their foreign earnings domestically. The amount of U.S. debt held by China still concerns me greatly. In 2011, ADM Michael Mullen said that the national debt is the greatest threat to our Nation.

♦How does China's holding of our debt impact our decisionmaking with regard to security? Particularly with security decisions in this increasingly volatile region?

Answer. U.S. decisionmaking and engagement in the Asia-Pacific region, as elsewhere in the world, is based on U.S. national security interests and priorities. China's U.S. Treasury holdings are not a factor in our security decisionmaking.

NEW CHINESE INVESTMENT BANK

China last year created the Asia Infrastructure Investment Bank to, "promote interconnectivity and integration in the region." It is clear that Asia has yawning gaps in infrastructure financing that must be addressed. Roads, bridges, ports, railroads, and airports will be key to spurring economic growth in the region. It has been widely reported that the U.S. lobbied other nations not to join the AIIB. However, the United Kingdom, Germany, France, and other Western nations have joined the AIIB.

41

Question (a). Can you explain to me why the United States chose not to sign up as a founding member?

Answer. I would refer you to the State Department on questions related to the Asia Infrastructure Investment Bank.

Question (b). Do you believe the United States should join the AIIB now?

Answer. I would refer you to the State Department on questions related to the Asia Infrastructure Investment Bank.

TRADE BALANCE

Question. China is currently the United States third-largest export market and biggest source of imports, making it the second-largest overall U.S. trading partner. In 2014, U.S. exports to, and imports from, China were an estimated $125 billion and $466 billion, respectively. According to the U.S. Bureau of Economic Analysis, cumulative Chinese foreign direct investment (FDI) in the United States by the end of 2013 was $8.1 billion, while cumulative U.S. FDI in China was $61.5 billion. At an estimated $341 billion in 2014, the U.S. trade deficit with China is significantly larger than its trade deficit with any other partner. I think that one problem we face now, is that we have gotten out of balance on the trade front with China. I am concerned that this lack of balance on trade is causing China to act out more aggressively.

♦I am curious to get your views, on the economic diplomacy here, if you think that increased trade and economic dependency between our two nations might ease China's recent military behavior?

Answer. President Obama has made clear that the United States welcomes a positive, cooperative, and comprehensive relationship with China. This includes positive economic, political, and military relations. However, I cannot speculate on the precise relationship between economic relations and Chinese military behavior.

JAPAN

In his address to Congress, Prime Minister Abe told us that Japan is, "resolved to take yet more responsibility for the peace and stability in the world." During his press conference with the Premier, President Obama reiterated, "our treaty commitment to Japan's security is absolute, and that Article 5 covers all territories under Japan's administration, including the Senkaku Islands . . . and the United States and Japan are united in our commitment to freedom of navigation, respect for international law, and the peaceful resolution of disputes without coercion."

Question (a). Mr. Shear, Mr. Russel, can you detail how the new security guidelines would affect a U.S.-Japanese response to Chinese encroachment against the Senkaku islands?

Answer. As reflected in the President's statement quoted above, the United States position on the Senkaku Islands is long-standing: we acknowledge that Japan administers the Senkaku Islands and has done so since the 1972 reversion of Okinawa to Japan. As such, the islands fall under Article V of the U.S.-Japan Treaty of Mutual Cooperation and Security. Article V provides that "[e]ach Party recognizes that an armed attack against either Party in the territories under the administration of Japan would be dangerous to its own peace and safety and declares that it would act to meet the common danger in accordance with its constitutional provisions and processes." However, we do not take a position on the question of ultimate sovereignty.

We continue to carry out our rebalance to the Asia-Pacific by dedicating more resources to the region in a way that is commensurate with the truly comprehensive nature of our engagement. The stronger U.S.-Japan Alliance cemented by the new Guidelines for U.S.-Japan Defense Cooperation is a success story of the rebalance strategy. The new guidelines also provide a framework for Japan to expand its contributions to international peace and security in concert with the United States and like-minded partners during the coming decades.

Question (b). In addition to the new guidelines, Japan has reinterpreted its Constitution to allow a right to collective self-defense. Can you describe Japan's goals in this ongoing reevaluation of its global role?

Answer. We welcome the Government of Japan's new policy regarding collective self-defense and related security activities. The U.S.-Japan alliance is one of our most important security partnerships. We, therefore, value efforts by Japan to strengthen our bilateral cooperation. We will continue to carry out our rebalance to the Asia-Pacific by dedicating more resources to the region in a way that is commensurate with the truly comprehensive nature of our engagement. The stronger U.S.-Japan Alliance cemented by the new Guidelines for U.S.-Japan Defense Cooperation is a success story of the rebalance strategy. The new guidelines also provide a framework for Japan to expand its contributions to international peace and security in concert with the United States and like-minded partners during the coming decades. In addition, we welcome Japan playing a greater international role in promoting peace and security, as demonstrated by its decisions to send reconstruction and support forces to Iraq and Kuwait, deploy peacekeepers to South Sudan and Haiti, conduct refueling activities in the Indian Ocean, and dispatch naval assets to counter piracy. We appreciate Japan's efforts to maintain openness and transparency throughout the implementation of this new policy. Japan wishes to build on its contributions to regional and global security, having demonstrated over the last 70 years an abiding commitment to peace, democracy, and the rule of law.

CHINA'S MILITARY MODERNIZATION

China recently announced that its defense budget would grow another 10 percent in 2015. Although official statistics are not reliable, a leading estimate suggests that Chinese defense spending sped past $200 billion per year in 2014, a sixfold increase over the course of 15 years. Meanwhile, the Pentagon's base budget has fallen by 14 percent over the past 5 years, and the 2015 Department of Defense report on military and security developments involving the People's Republic of China finds that ''China's military modernization has the potential to reduce core U.S. military technological advantages.''

Question (a). Mr. Shear, Mr. Russel, in light of these facts, do you agree that the regional balance of power continues to shift in China's favor?

Answer. As you note, DOD's 2015 Report on Military and Security Developments in the People's Republic of China highlights China's extensive investments in capabilities that have the potential to erode U.S. military technological advantages over time. However, the United States has abiding areas of strength that no other country—including China—can match: from our unrivaled ability to innovate, to our unparalleled operational experience, and our extensive network of alliances and partnerships in the region. As part of President Obama's rebalance strategy, the Department of Defense is modernizing our alliances and partnerships; we are enhancing our defense posture to be more geographically distributed, operationally resilient, and politically sustainable; we are moving key capabilities and assets forward to the Asia-Pacific region; and we are investing in new capabilities that will be especially relevant to the security environment in the future. In short, as Secretary Carter has stated, the United States ''will remain the principal security power in the Asia-Pacific for decades to come.''

Question (b). Has it already reached a point where China has a military advantage over the United States in regional waters, inside the ''first island chain''?

Answer. No. As Secretary Carter has said, although we face challenges to our technological superiority, it will take years for any country to build the kind of military capability the United States possesses today. And in the meantime, we will not be standing still. The Department has committed to moving our finest capabilities and assets forward to the Asia-Pacific region, and we are investing in new capabilities that will be especially relevant to the security environment in the future. We are mindful of several countries' growing areas of military strength and will continue to make the investments necessary to ensure that we manage security competition from a position of strength.

Question (c). Is it possible to begin shifting the balance back in our favor while sequestration remains in place?

Answer. We are doing what we can with the funds and authorities we have at this time. We would, of course, welcome additional funds and authorities to do more.

Question (d). Does the continuing shift in China's favor undermine the U.S. ability to deter provocative behavior, such as China's intimidation tactics in the South and East China Seas?

Answer. No. The United States is taking active steps to deter aggression and coercion in the Asia-Pacific region. The Department of Defense has committed to moving our finest capabilities and assets forward to the Asia-Pacific region, and we are investing in new capabilities that will be especially relevant to the security environment in the future. We are also modernizing our alliances and partnerships to ensure they can meet the challenges of the Asia-Pacific region's dynamic security environment. Finally, we are adopting a more geographically distributed, operationally resilient, and politically sustainable defense posture that will bolster our persistent presence across the region, especially in Southeast Asia. As Secretary Carter has stated, the United States will ''remain the principal security power in the Asia-Pacific for decades to come.''

CHINESE SHIP-BUILDING

In the 2015 posture statement for U.S. Pacific Command, Admiral Locklear chronicled China's extensive military modernization programs. It is pursuing an ''aggressive shipbuilding program to produce and field advanced frigates, destroyers, and the first in-class cruiser-sized warship,'' and will soon begin construction of its first indigenously-produced aircraft carrier.

Question (a). Mr. Shear, can you summarize what capabilities these new platforms will have in comparison to the U.S. Navy, and those of our regional allies?

Answer. As we have noted in our Annual Report to Congress on Military and Security Developments Involving the People's Republic of China, China's ambitious naval modernization program is producing a more technologically advanced and flexible force that now consists of the largest naval fleet in Asia. The United States continues to closely monitor these trends. While I cannot provide a comparative assessment of U.S. and Chinese naval capabilities, I would note that the United States is making significant investments in those capabilities most relevant to the Asia-Pacific security environment and we are committed to moving our finest capabilities forward to the region. As Secretary Carter has stated, the United States will ''remain the principal security power in the Asia-Pacific for decades to come.''

Question (b). To what extent will China's new naval capabilities facilitate its efforts to enforce its claims in the South and East China Seas?

Answer. To date, China has used its government controlled, civilian maritime law-enforcement agencies in maritime disputes and uses the PLA Navy in an overwatch capacity in case of escalation. The Chinese Coast Guard is rapidly increasing its total force level, adding new, larger patrol ships and craft as well as helicopters and UAVs. In the next decade, a new force of civilian law enforcement ships will afford China the capability to patrol more robustly in the East China Sea and the South China Sea. The PLA assets you mention could play a role in a situation where a maritime dispute escalates militarily. These assets could also be used to augment PLA presence operations in the region, for signaling and naval diplomacy.

CHINA'S PARTICIPATION IN RIMPAC

Question (a). Some U.S. lawmakers and military leaders have expressed their hope that the administration would cancel China's invitation to attend next year's RIMPAC military exercises.

♦Mr. Shear, in light of China's continued regional aggression, can you explain why China should be invited to participate in next year's exercise?

Answer. We invited China to the Rim of the Pacific (RIMPAC) exercise to demonstrate positive standards of multilateral security partnership, to advance cooperative approaches to common security challenges, and to increase transparency and mutual understanding. This exercise also integrates China into a cooperative multilateral forum, demonstrating the standards we seek to promote in the region. The exercise provides an opportunity for the United States, China, and countries throughout the Asia-Pacific region to put into practice the key tenets of operational safety that are essential to ensuring that tactical misunderstandings do not escalate into crises.

China's involvement will be scoped appropriately, based on our engagement objectives to increase cooperative capacity in areas of mutual interest, such disaster relief, humanitarian assistance, and counterpiracy. Of course, all engagements with the People's Liberation Army are carefully considered and reviewed for compliance with relevant law, policies, and regulations. As with all defense engagements, we continuously review military-to-military activities to assess their appropriateness and consistency with U.S. objectives. We may modify our engagement decisions based on evolving circumstances.

Question (b). What does the fact that China sent an intelligence vessel to monitor the 2014 RIMPAC exercises when it was invited to participate in them say about China's distrust of its neighbors and the United States?

Answer. We agree that it was odd for China to send an intelligence ship to observe its participation in the Rim of the Pacific (RIMPAC) exercise last year. However, it is important to note that the DONGDIAO-class vessel that China sent to conduct such operations followed international law and norms. The U.S. Navy conducts military operations in waters beyond the territorial seas of coastal nations around the world, and China is permitted to do the same.